Adult Coloring Books For Relaxation
Mandalas
Vol 2
Ravi Collection

Kai Loren

DEDICATION

This book is dedicated to my Lou. I will never forget all the fun adventures we have gone on together! From New Jersey to Alaska, Egypt to England, with you there is never a dull moment! But of all our adventures, the best was when we've just been. May you never lose your curiosity and zest for life. Love you more than you'll ever know.

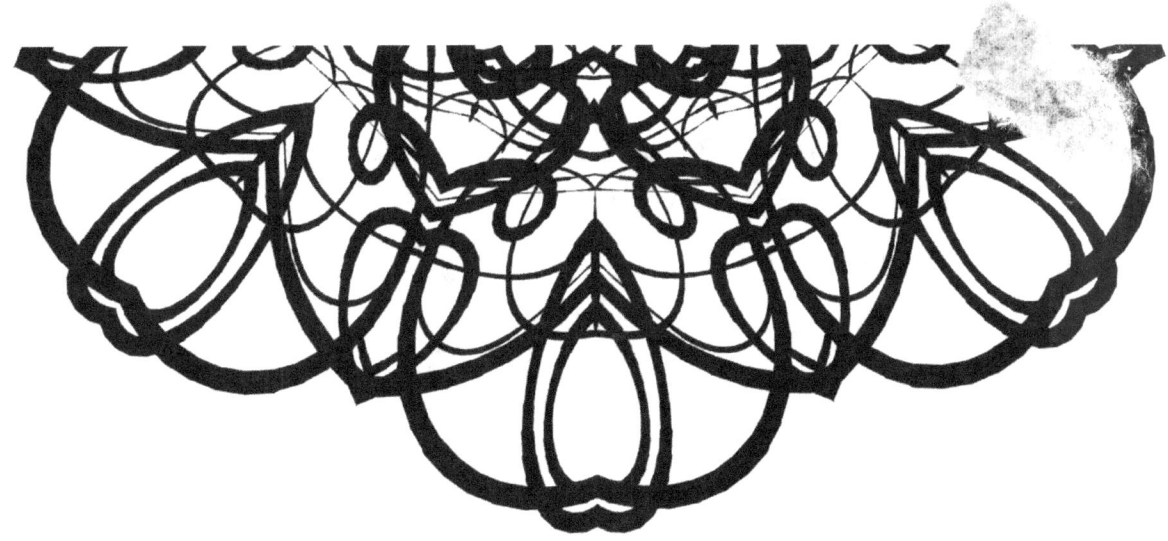

INTRODUCTION

Dictionary.com defines a mandala (MUHN-da-la) as "art of any of various designs symbolizing the universe, usually circular, and a symbol expressing a person's striving for unity of the self." Mandala is translated from ancient Indian Sanskrit to mean circle. These particular circles are powerful symbols that have been used by different cultures for thousands of years to represent balance, the circle of life, and a sense of unity and connection with all things.

The simple act of coloring in the 50 mandalas found throughout this book will help you enjoy some real therapeutic and physical benefits, including:

• Reduced stress and anxiety

• A sense of well-being

• Increased focus

• Increased creativity

• Reduced blood pressure

How does this work? Coloring forces your mind to focus on the task at hand -filing in the mandala- which doesn't leave room for it to focus on stress, worry, and fear. The reduction of these negative thoughts creates a sense of balance that's strengthened by the inherent meditative quality of the mandala. After spending just a short time coloring and letting your meditative mind wander, you find yourself living a life that's happier, healthier, and more in tune with the world around you. A clear mind and a healthy body are just a meditation away, so pick up your pencil and set your mind free.

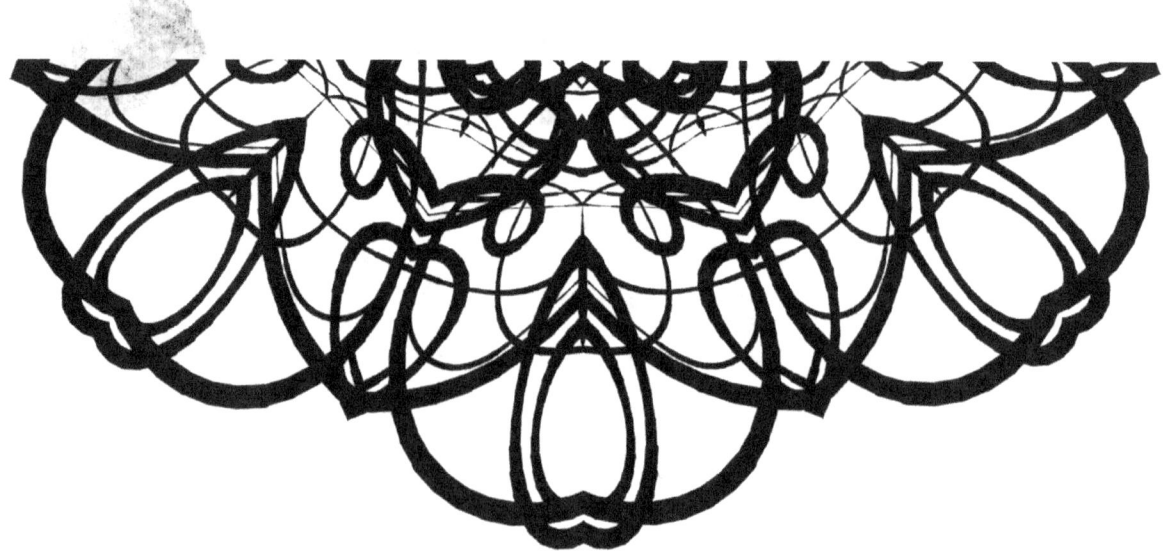

HOW TO USE THIS BOOK

Browse through the book and stop when you come across a mandala that speaks to you. Your subconscious mind knows what it needs and the mandala you pick will be the meditative tool that's right for the moment. Keep in mind that some mandalas can be colored relatively quickly, while others are more complex and will require more time. Think about how much time you have available. Do you want to finish the coloring in one sitting? Or are you happy to complete it over time?

Choosing your colors is a very personal thing and no one can tell you what colors should or shouldn't be used for any specific mandala. If you want to lay out your crayons or colored pencils in front of you and pick them up at random, that's okay. Or you can plan out the colors that you'll use based on your mood or preferences. Various colors can represent different things, for example:

• White = purity, innocence, positivity

• Red = passion, strength, power, danger

• Orange = enthusiasm, happiness, creativity

• Yellow = energy, intelligence, joy

• Green = growth, harmony, fertility

• Blue = loyalty, wisdom, truth

• Violet = nobility, wealth, ambition

Of course, sometimes a color is just a color, but looking at the symbolism of the colors you choose can give you a peak into your subconscious mind.

Each mandala you color will be a unique expression of yourself, so set your cares aside, and start coloring.

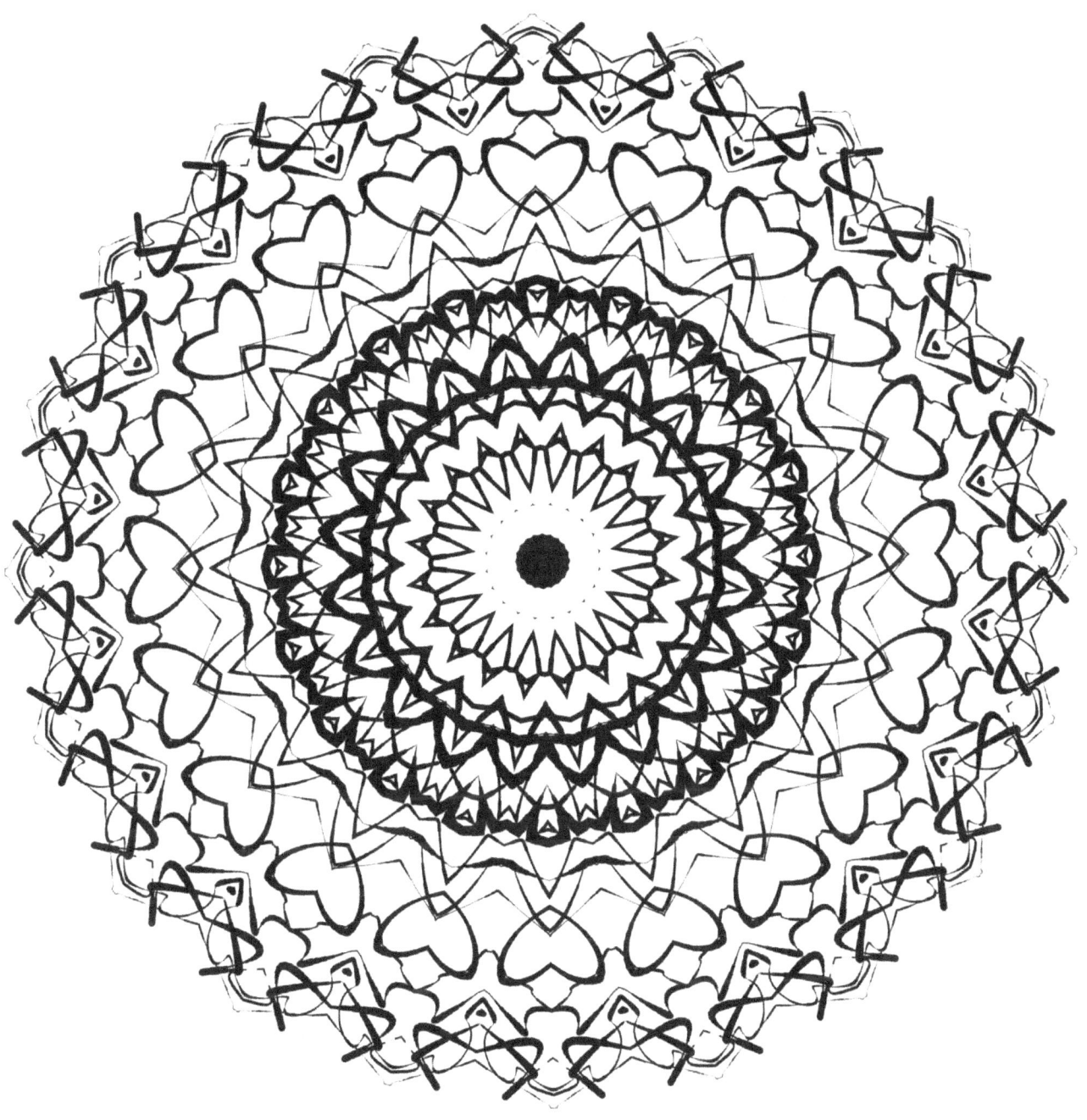

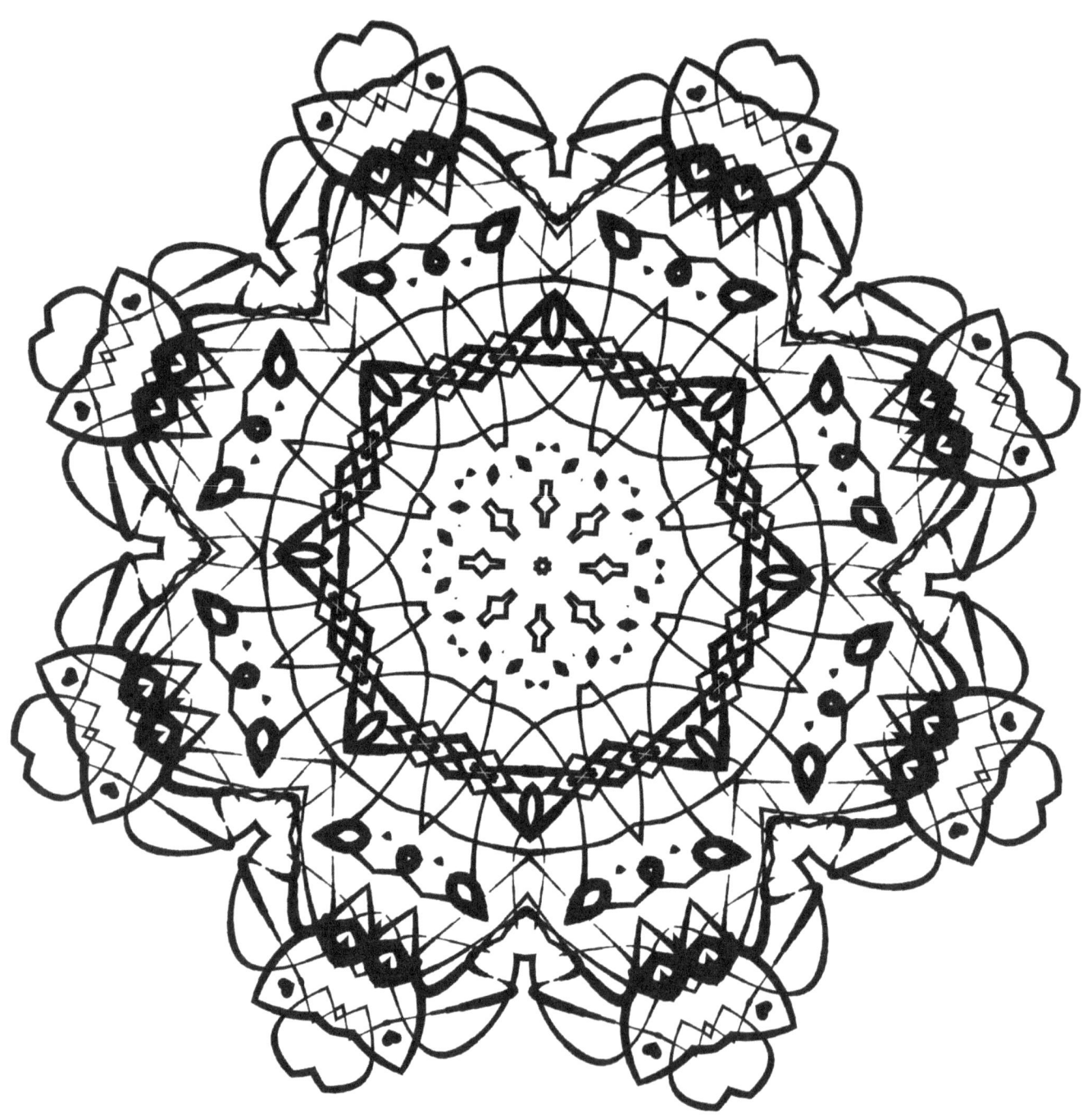

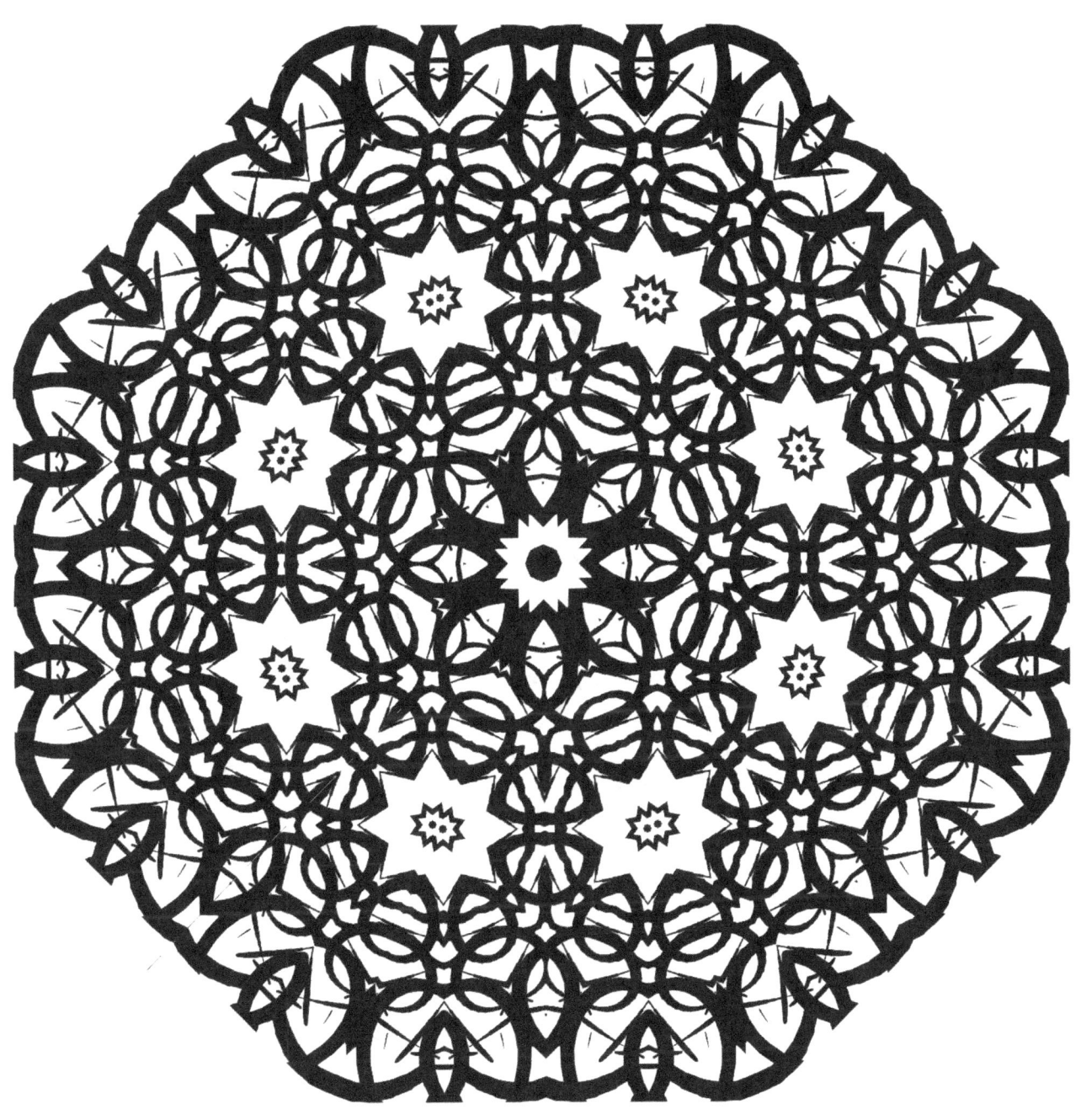

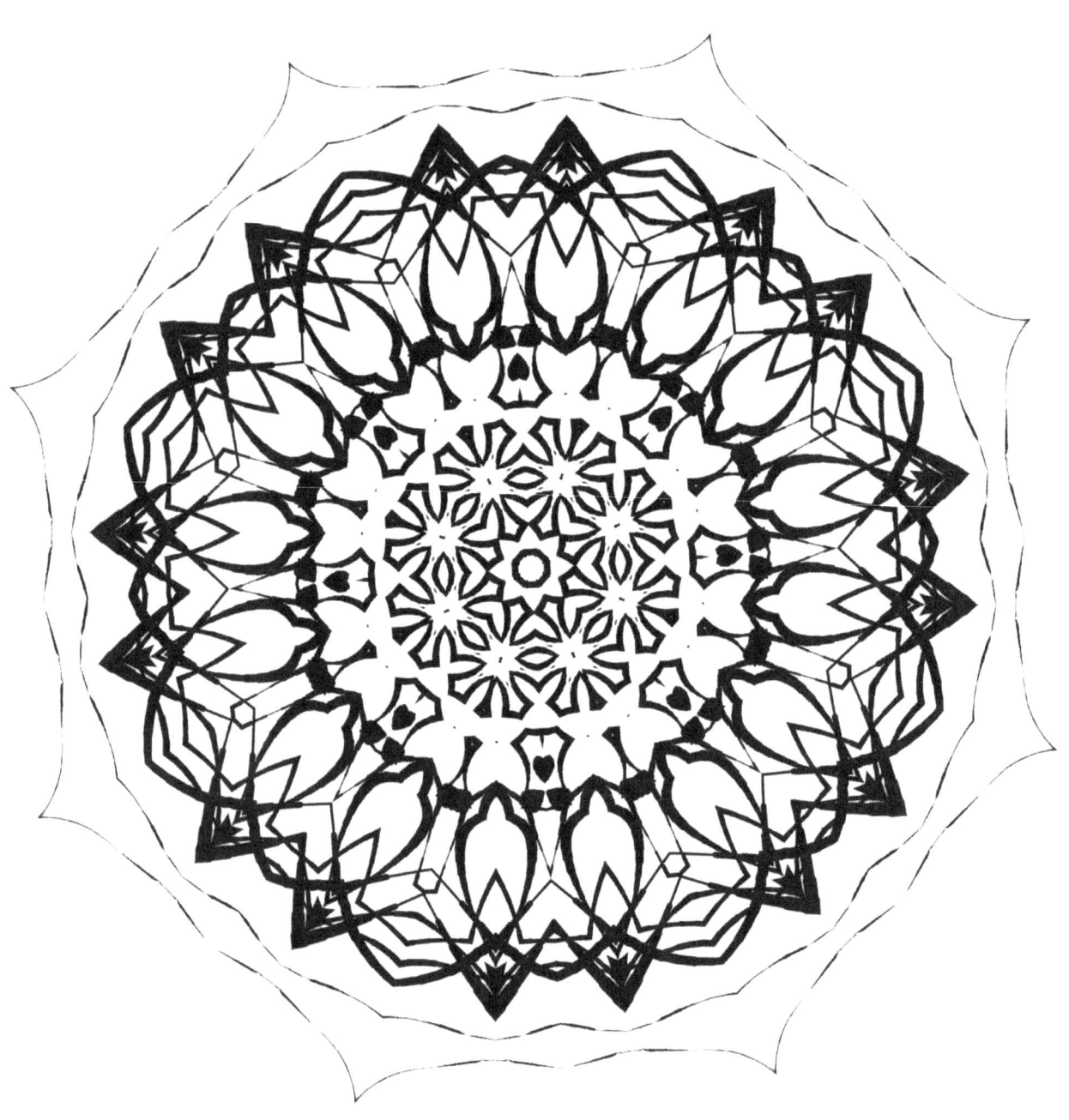

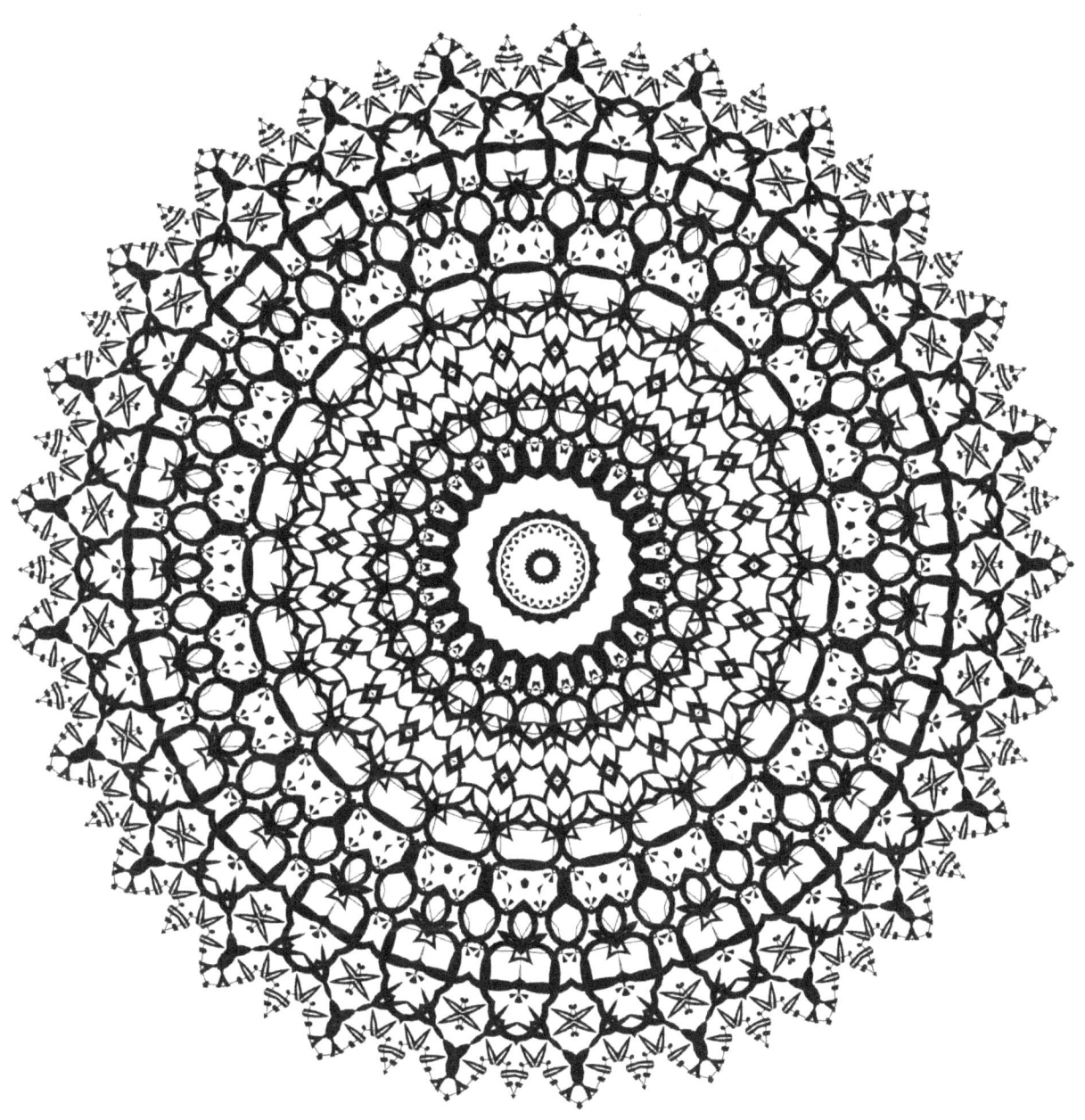

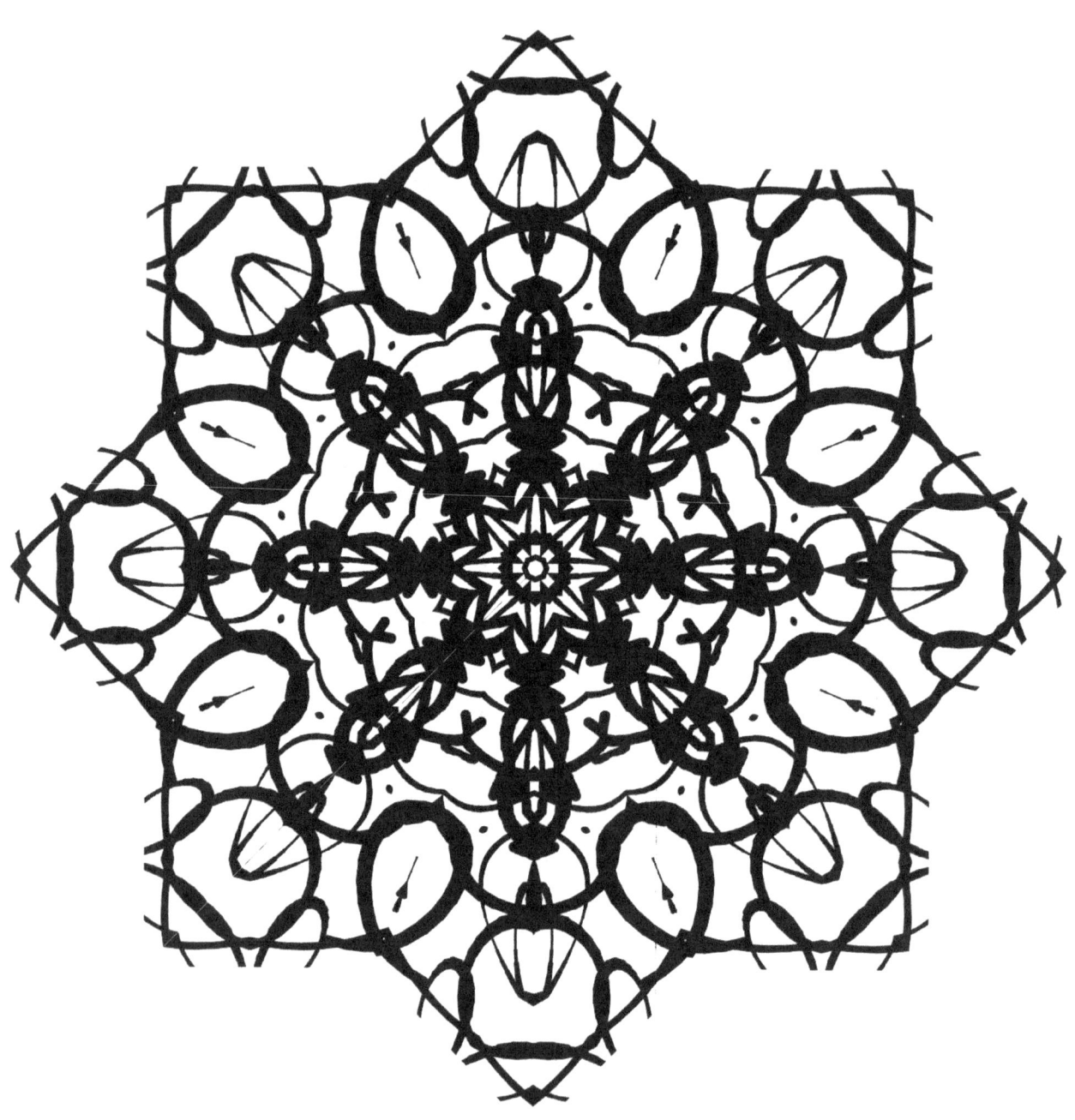

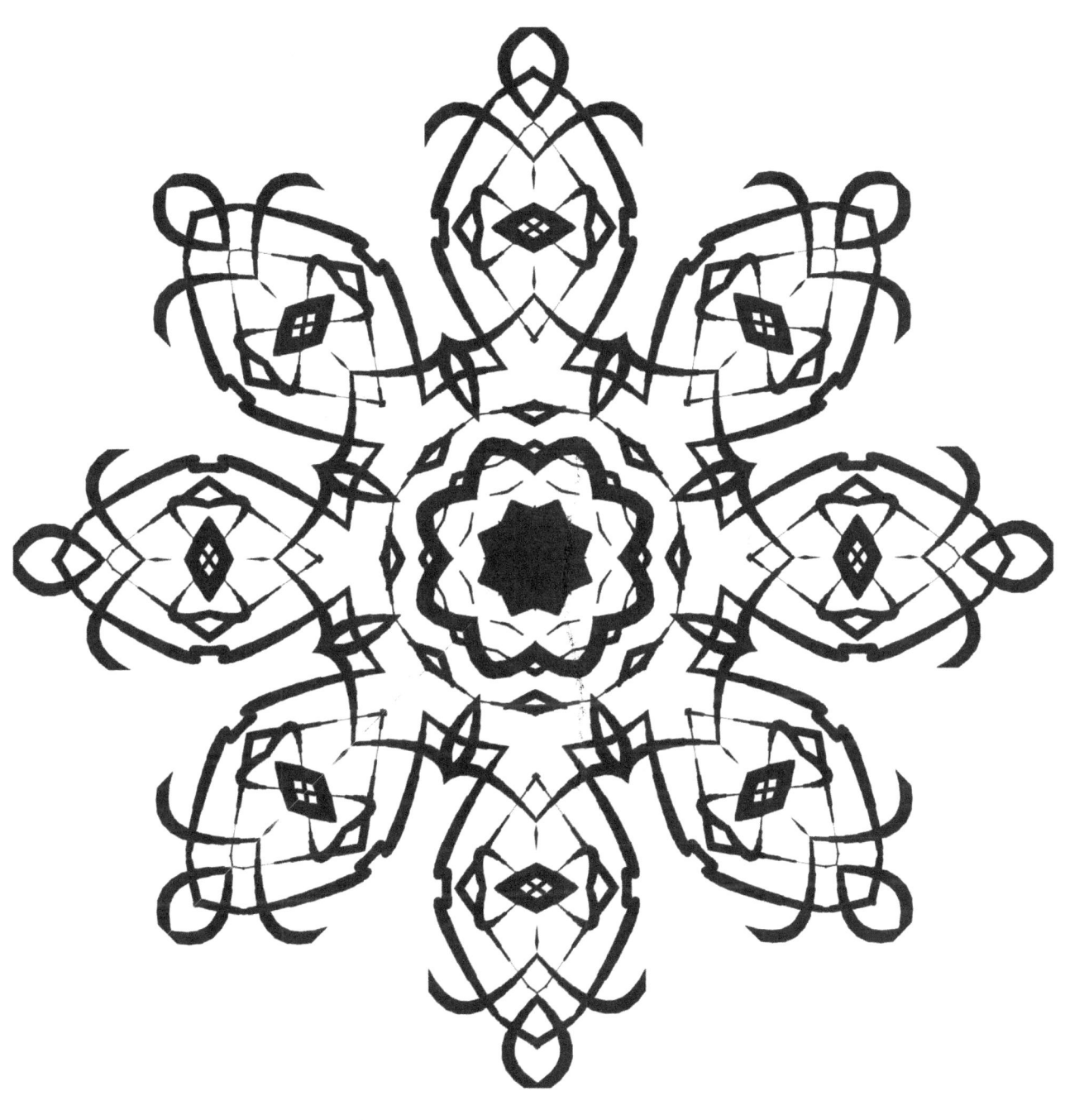

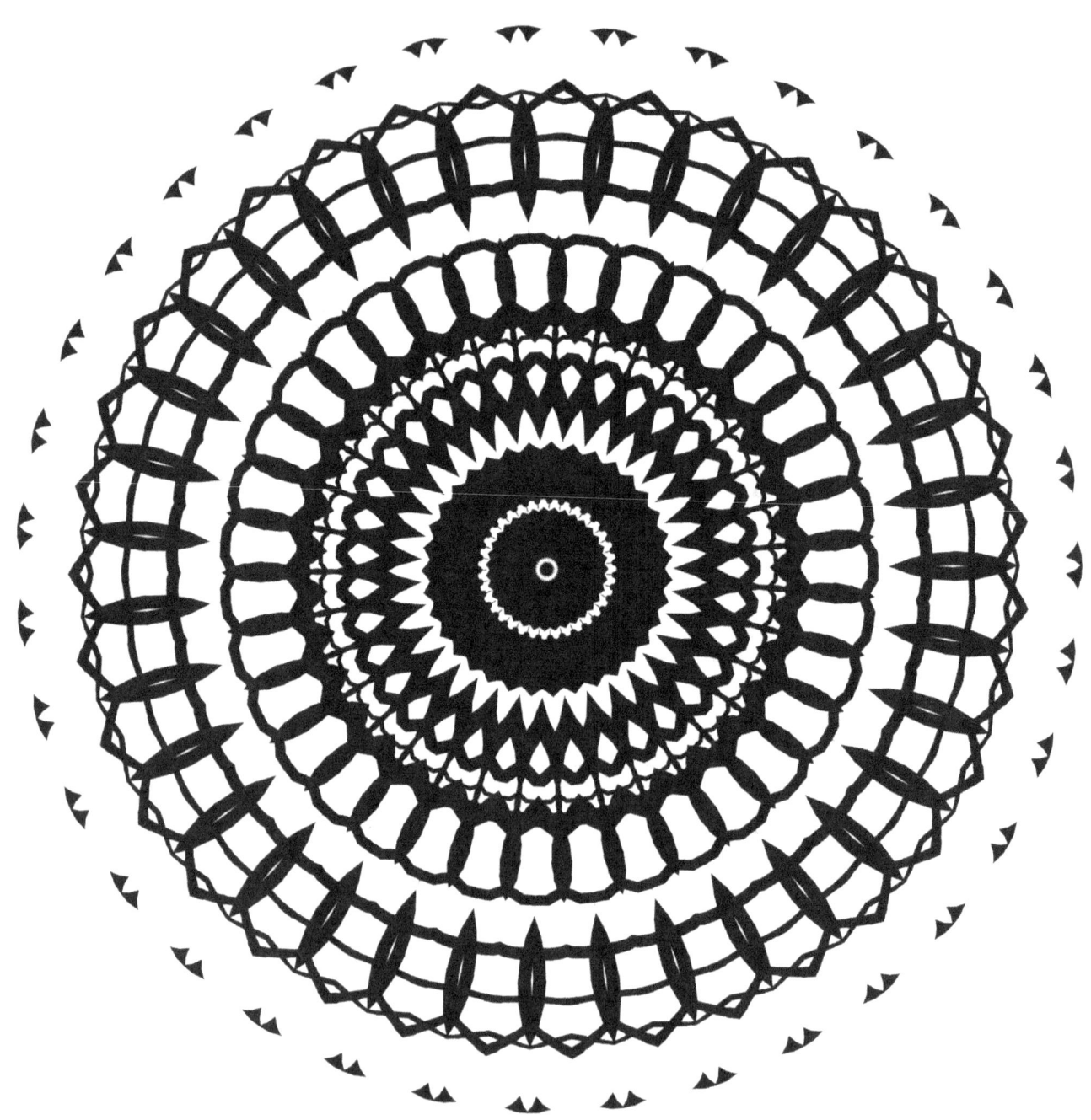

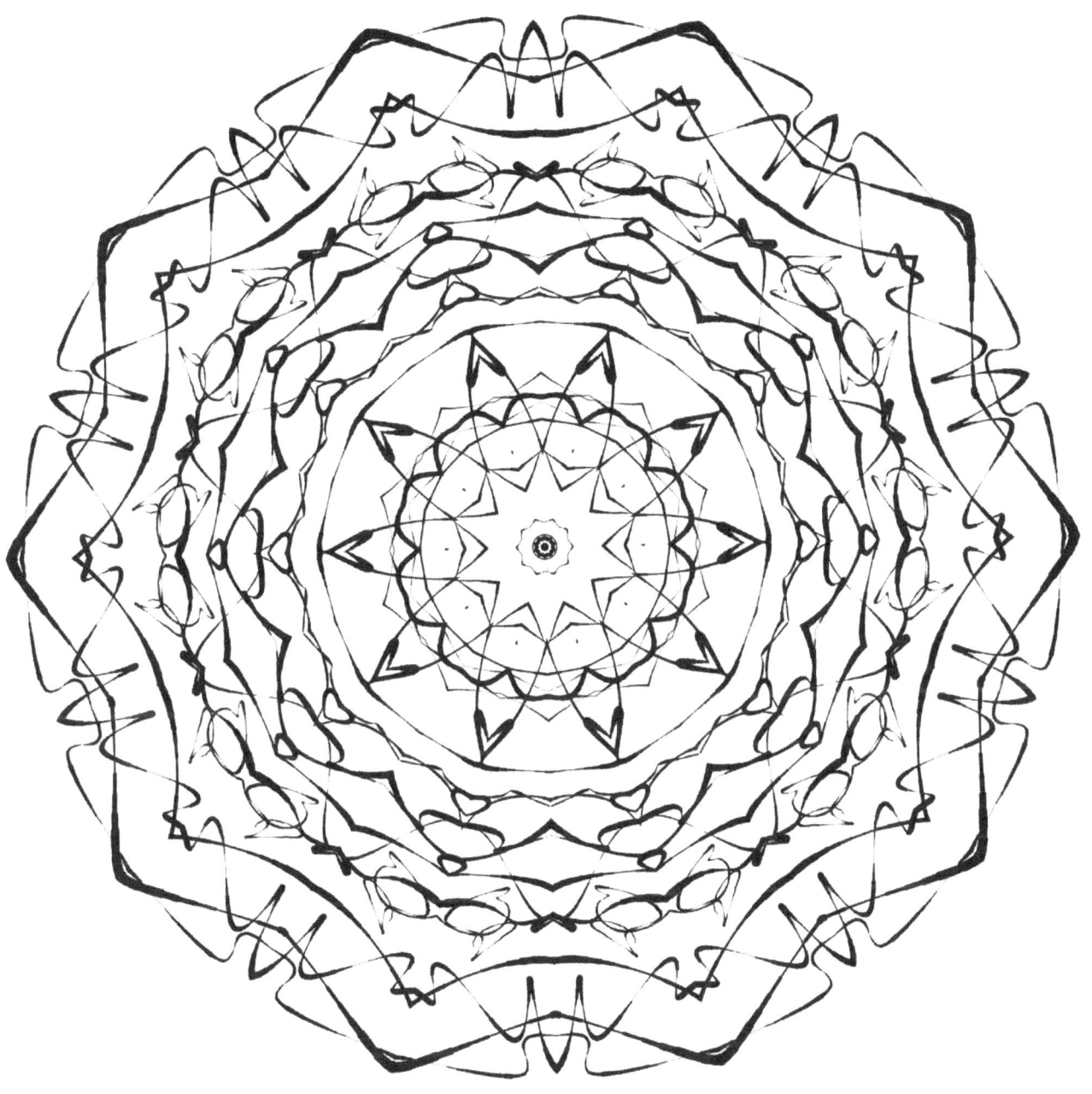

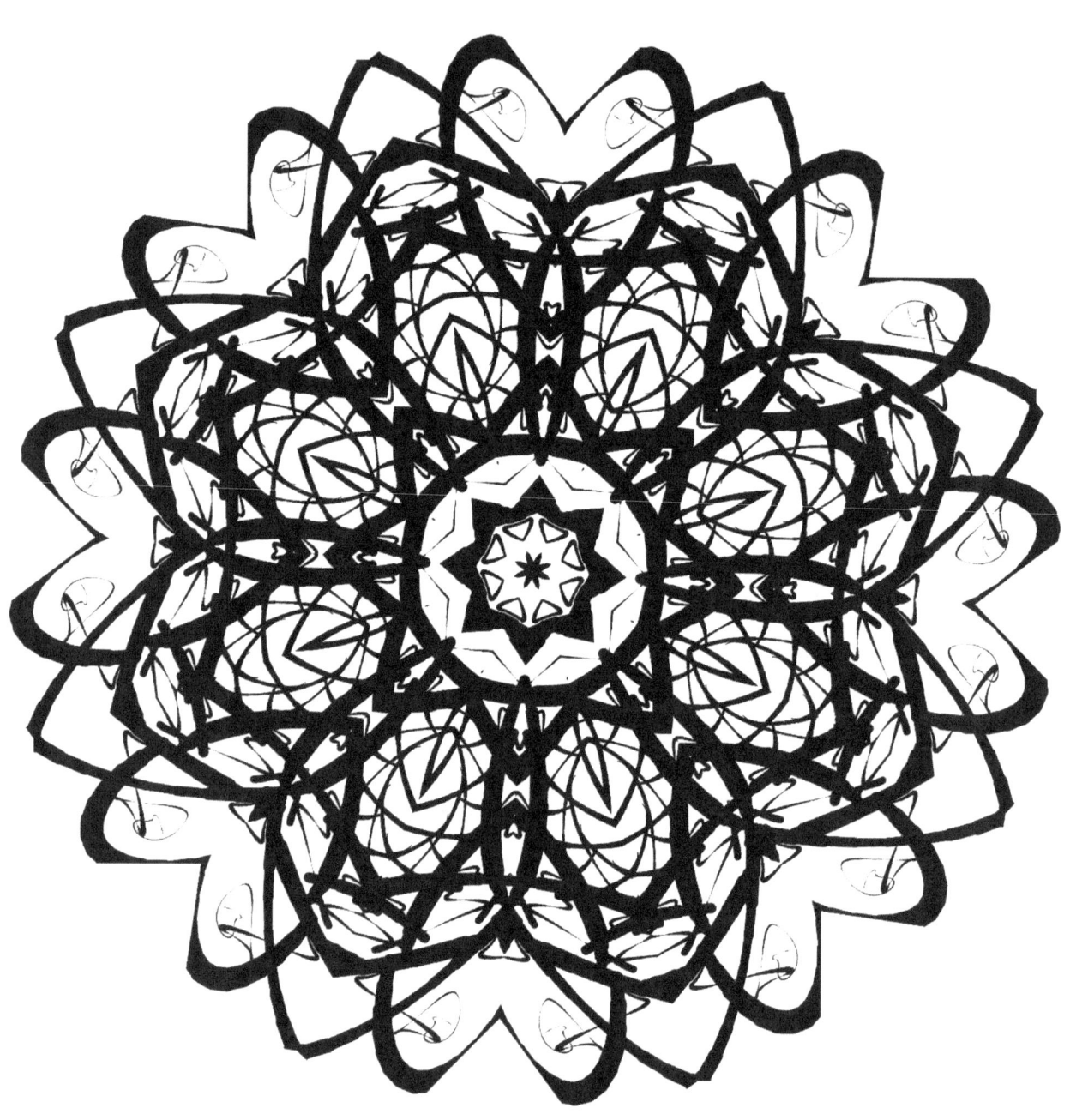

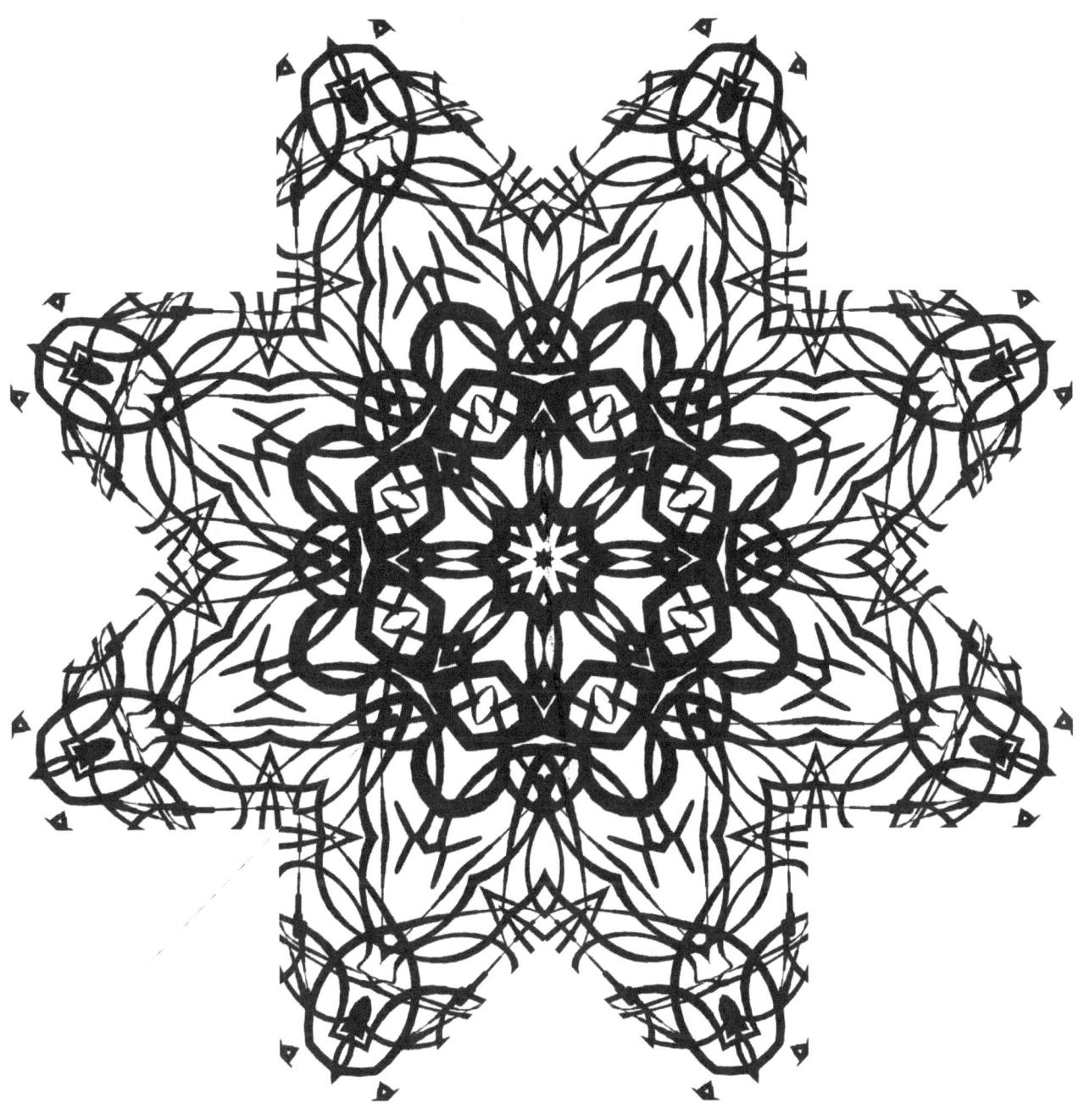

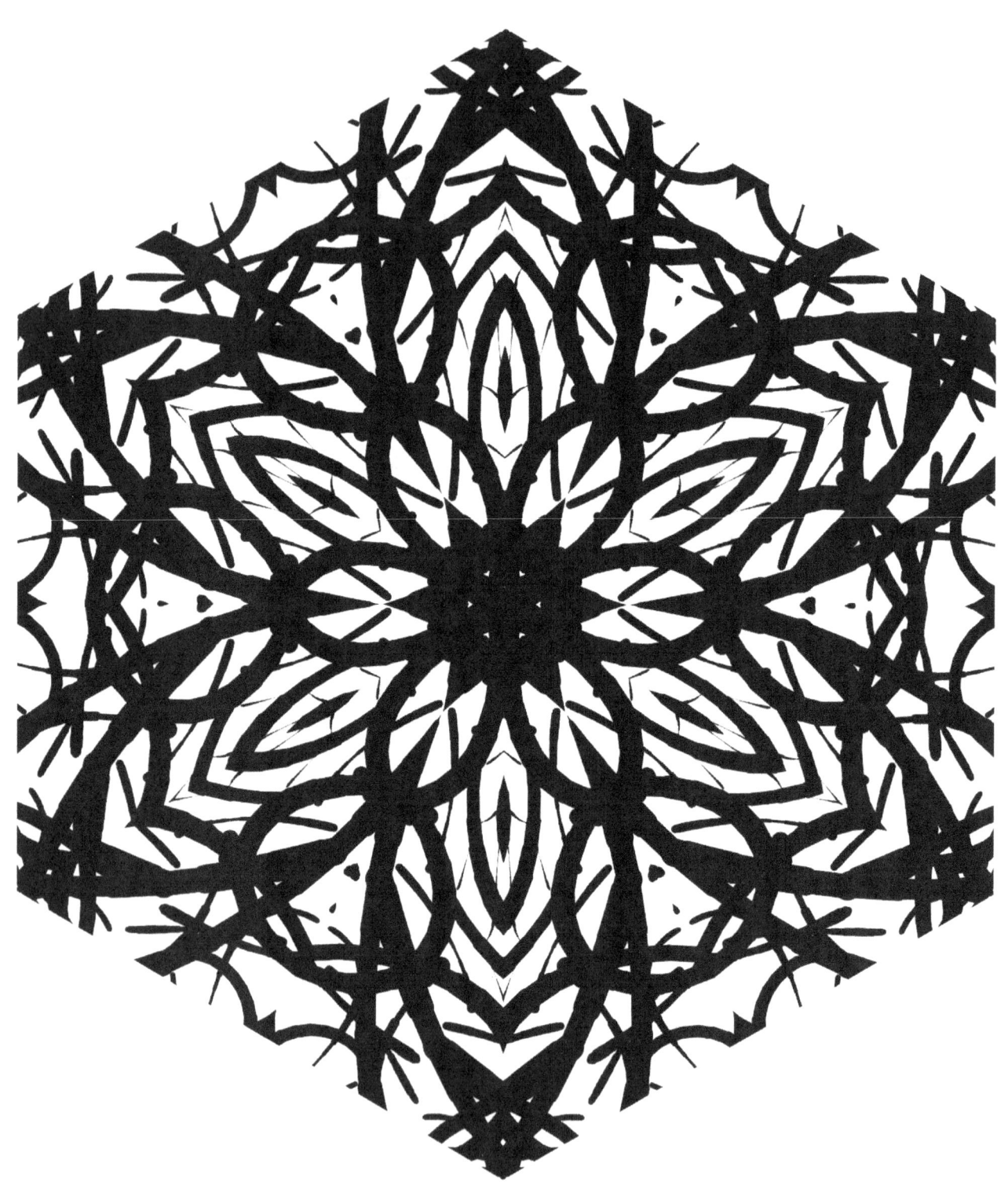

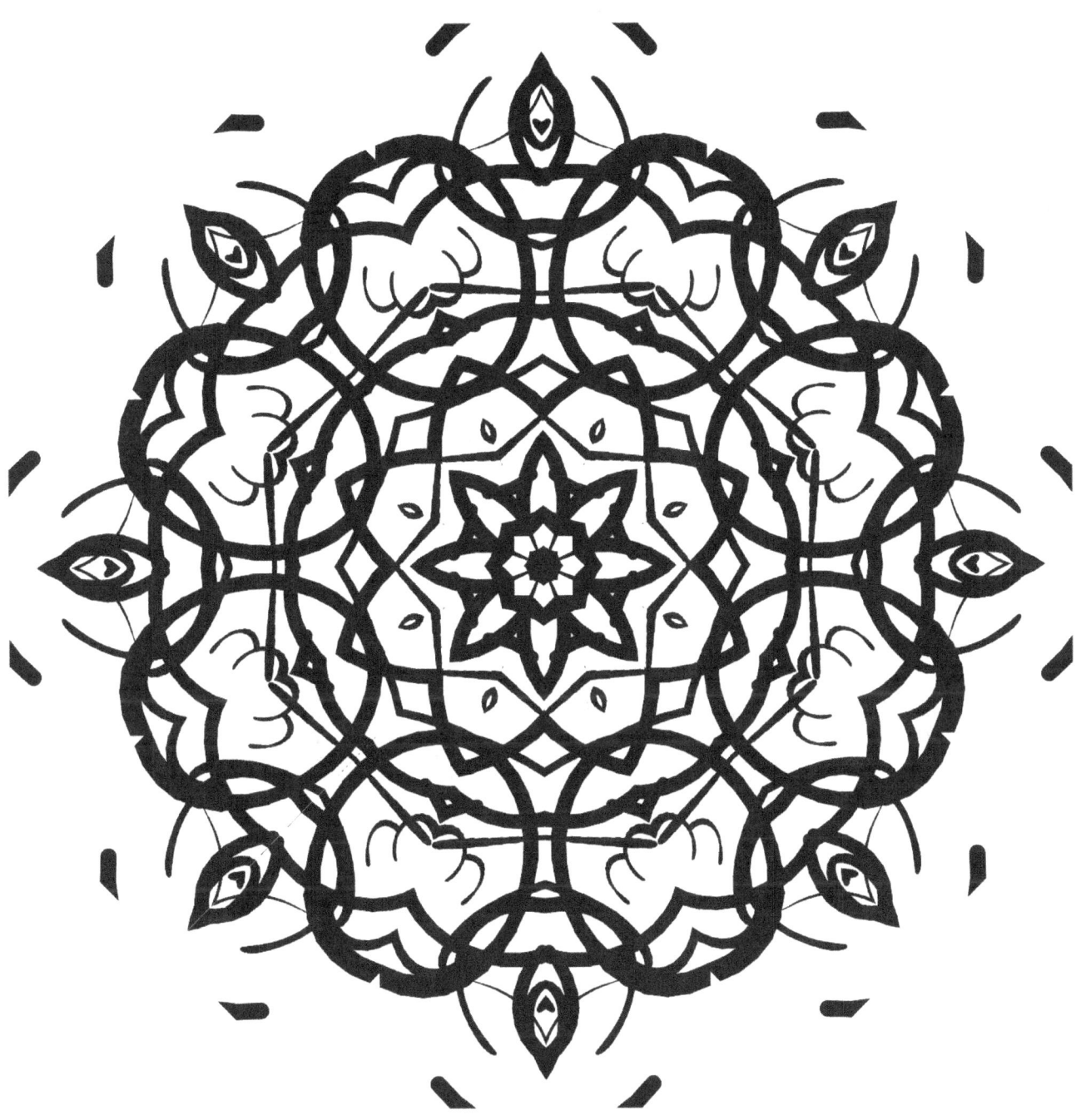

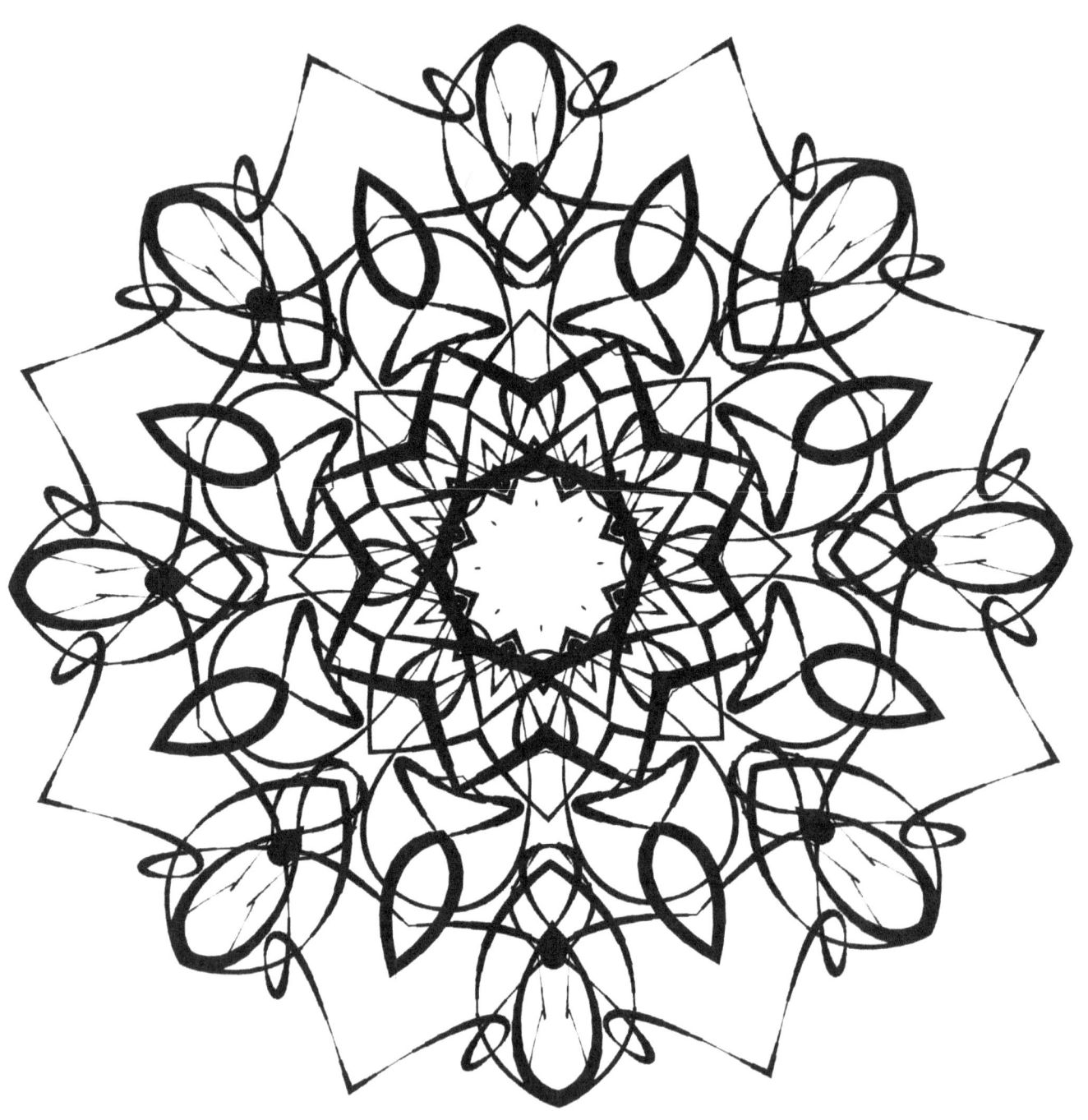

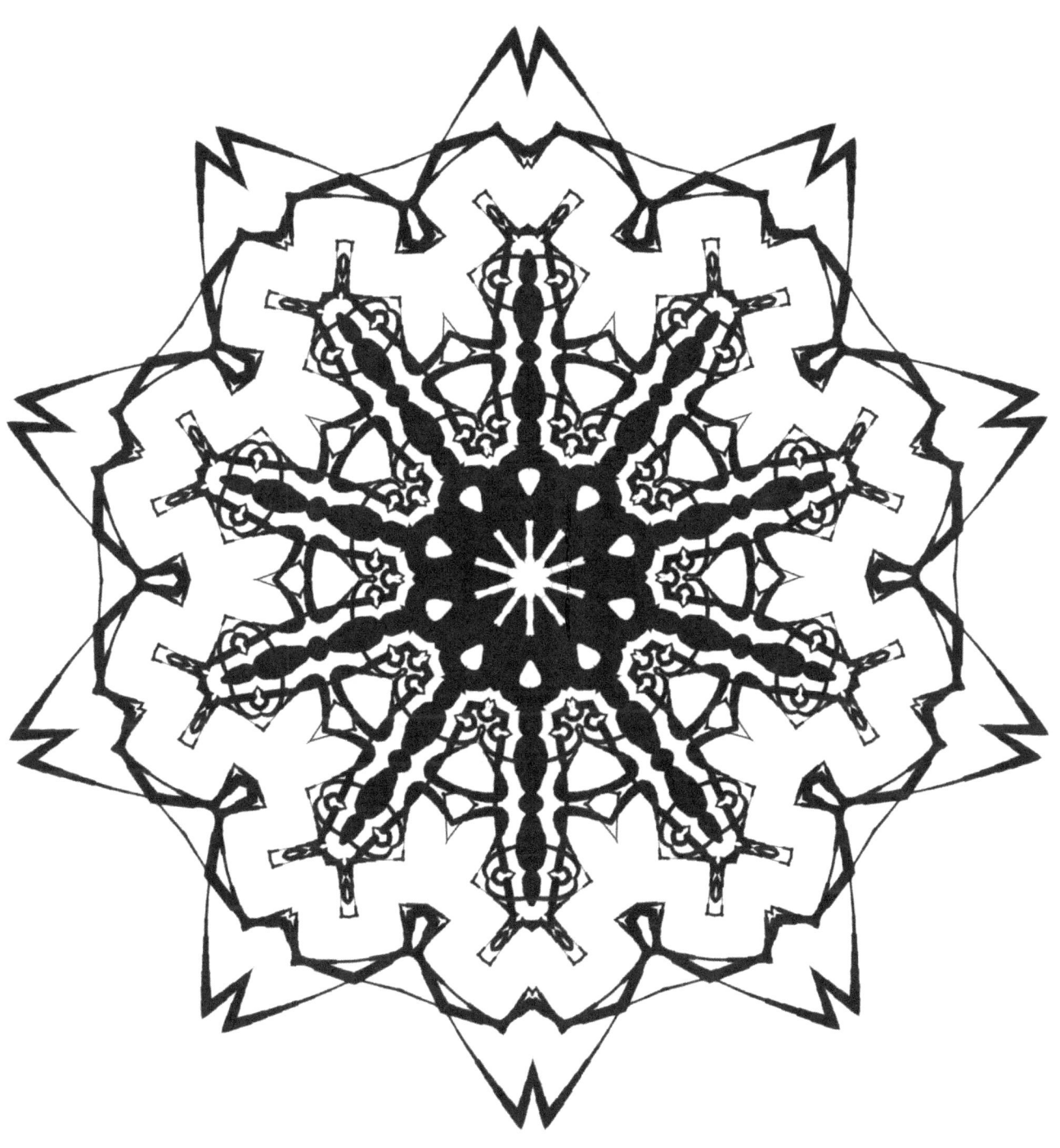

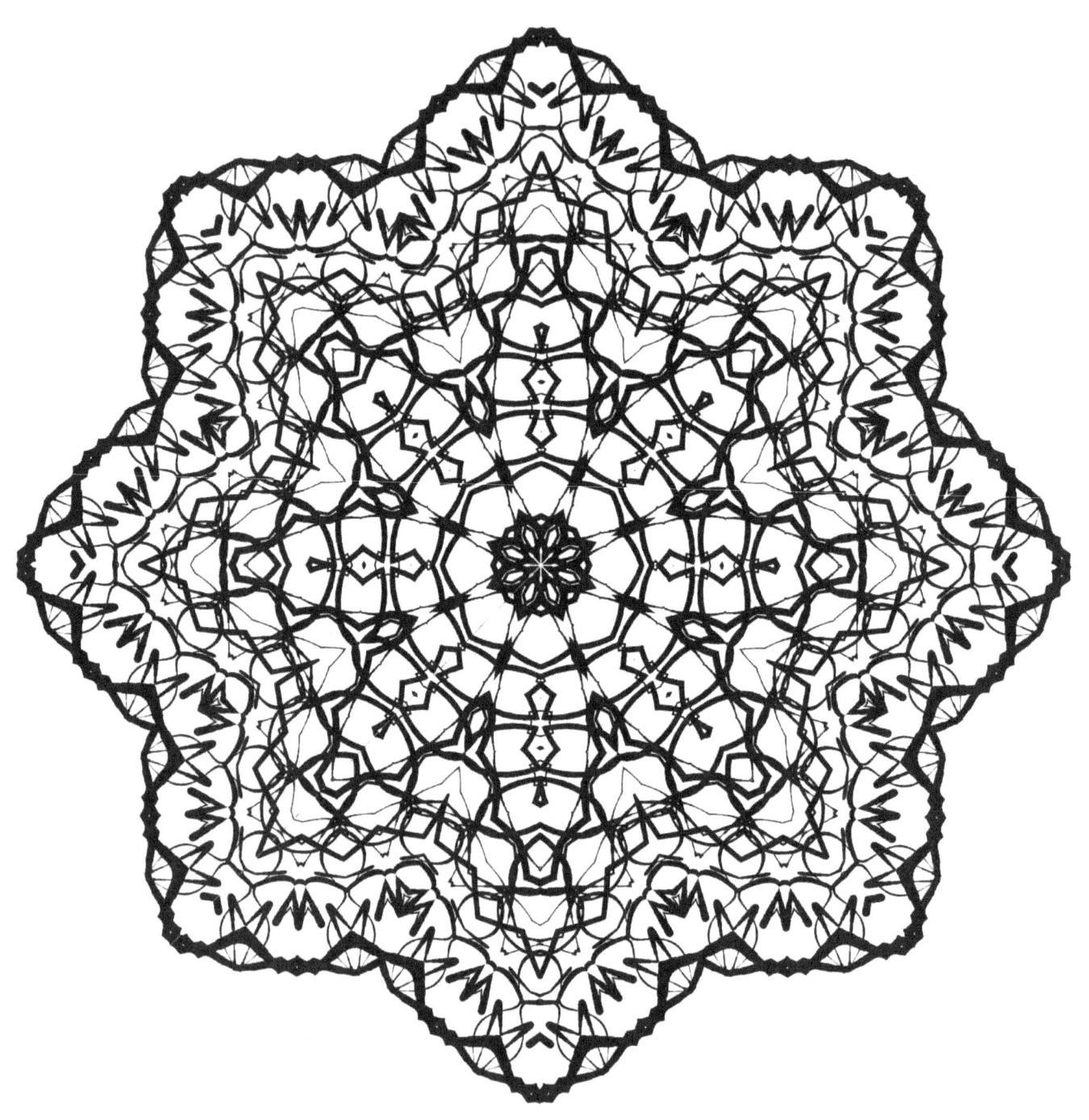

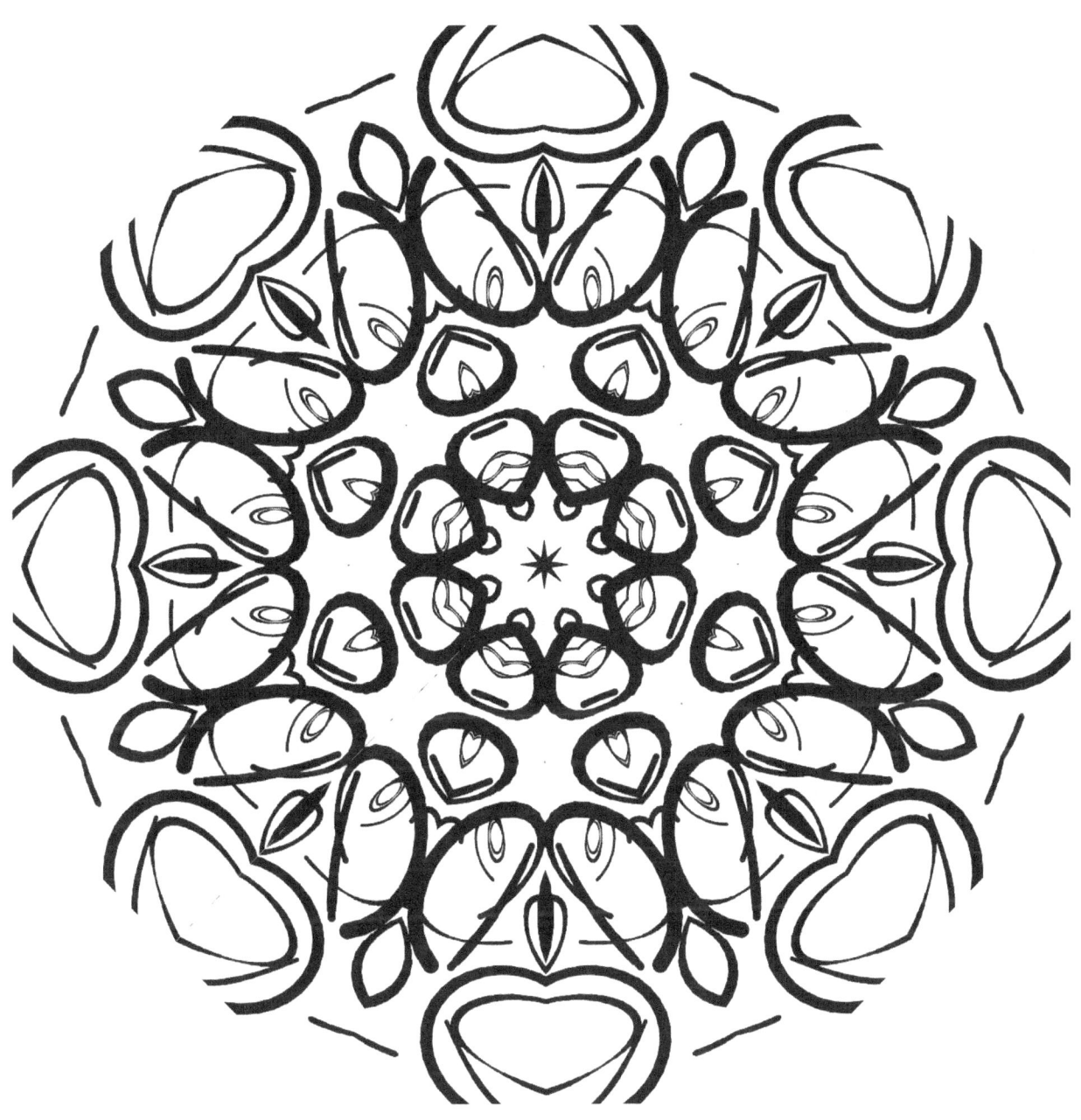

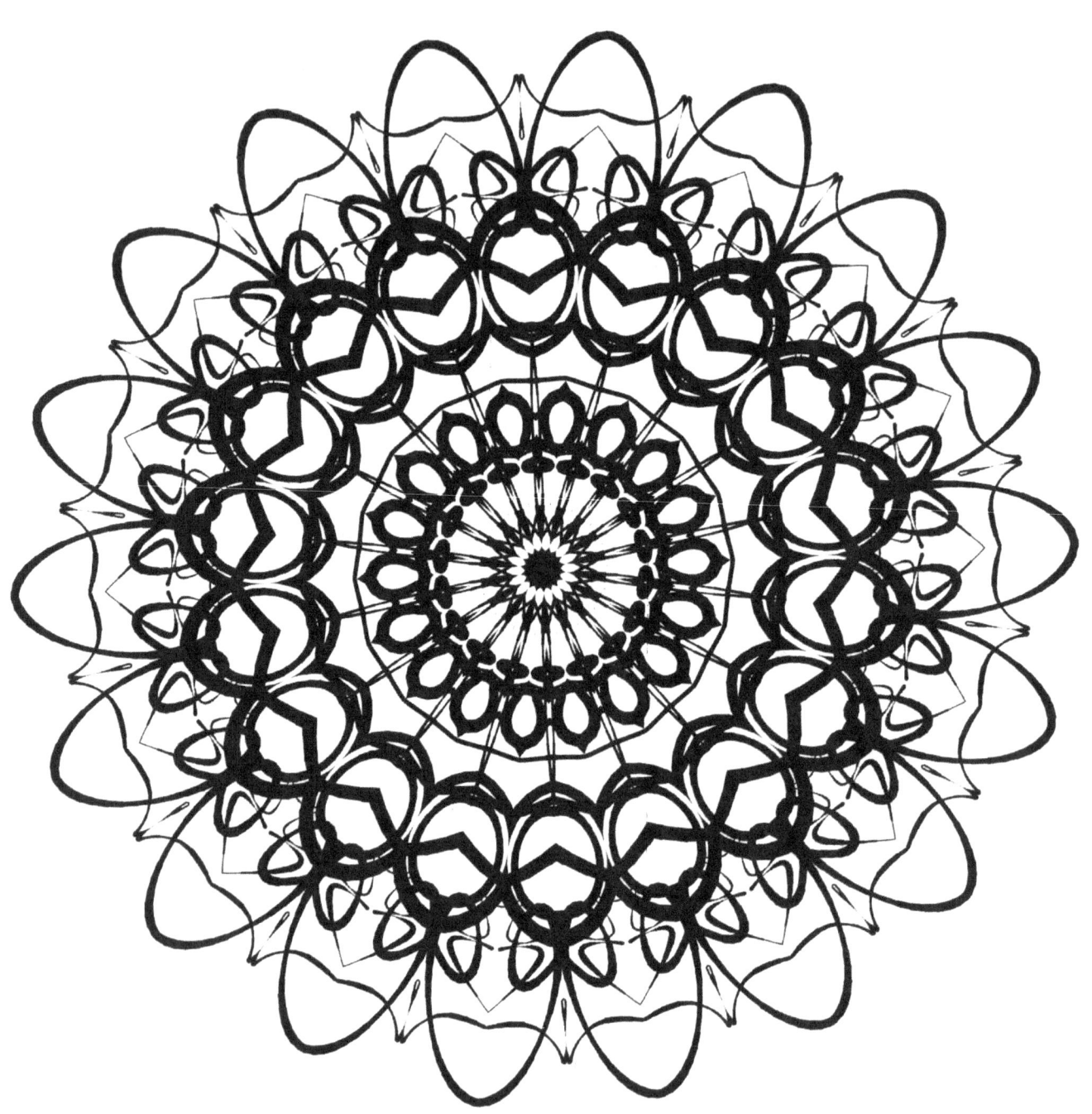

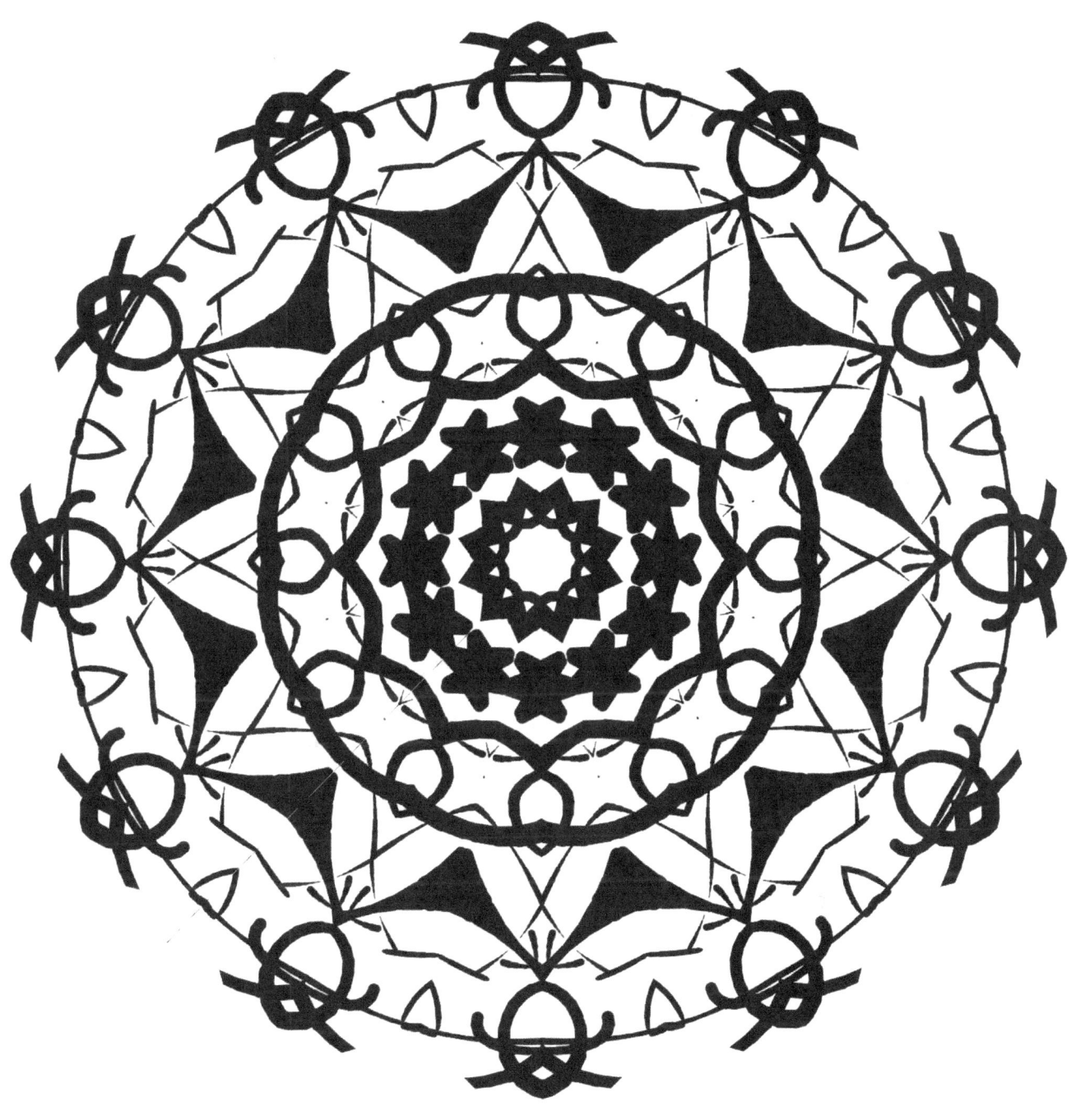

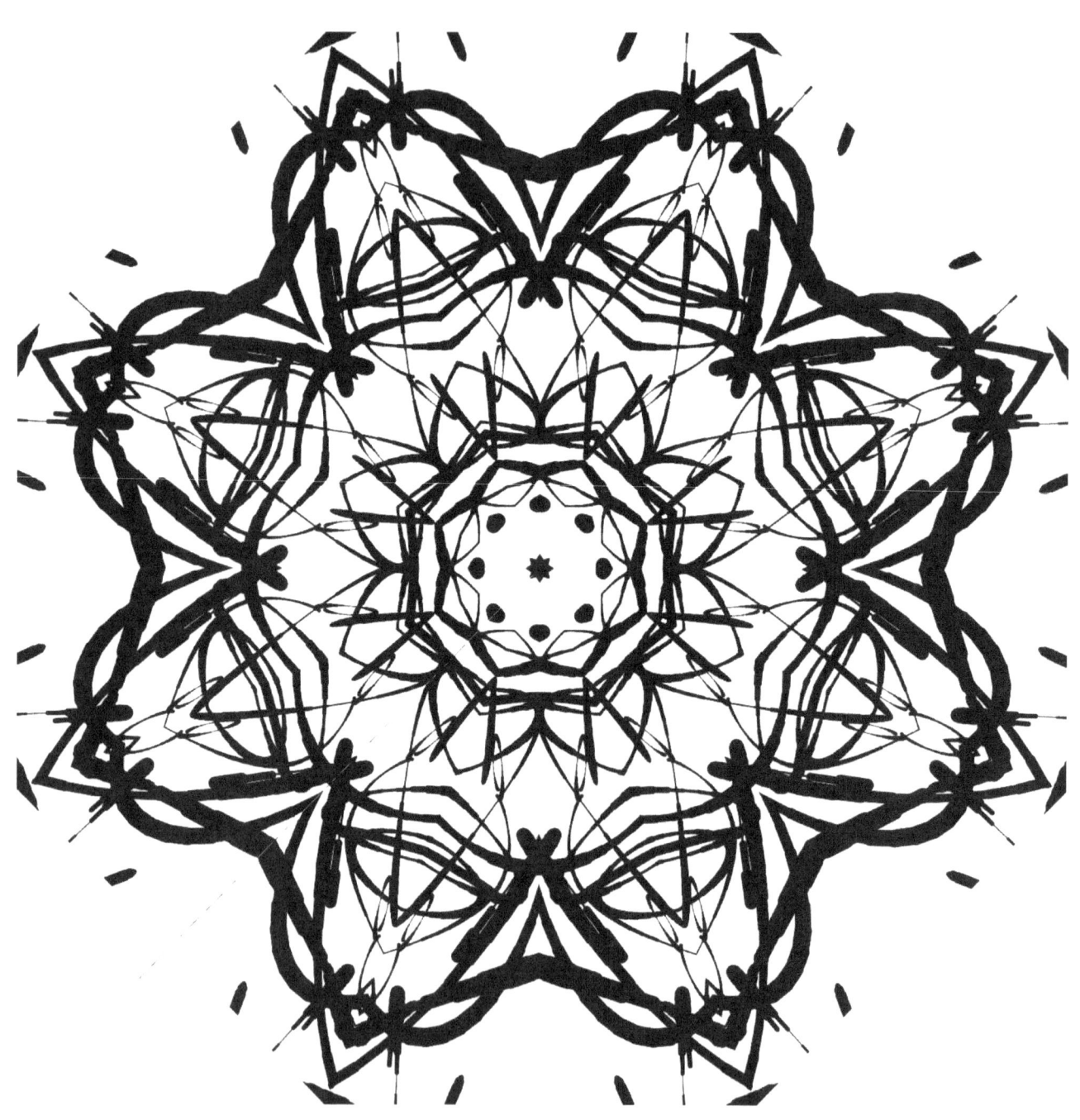

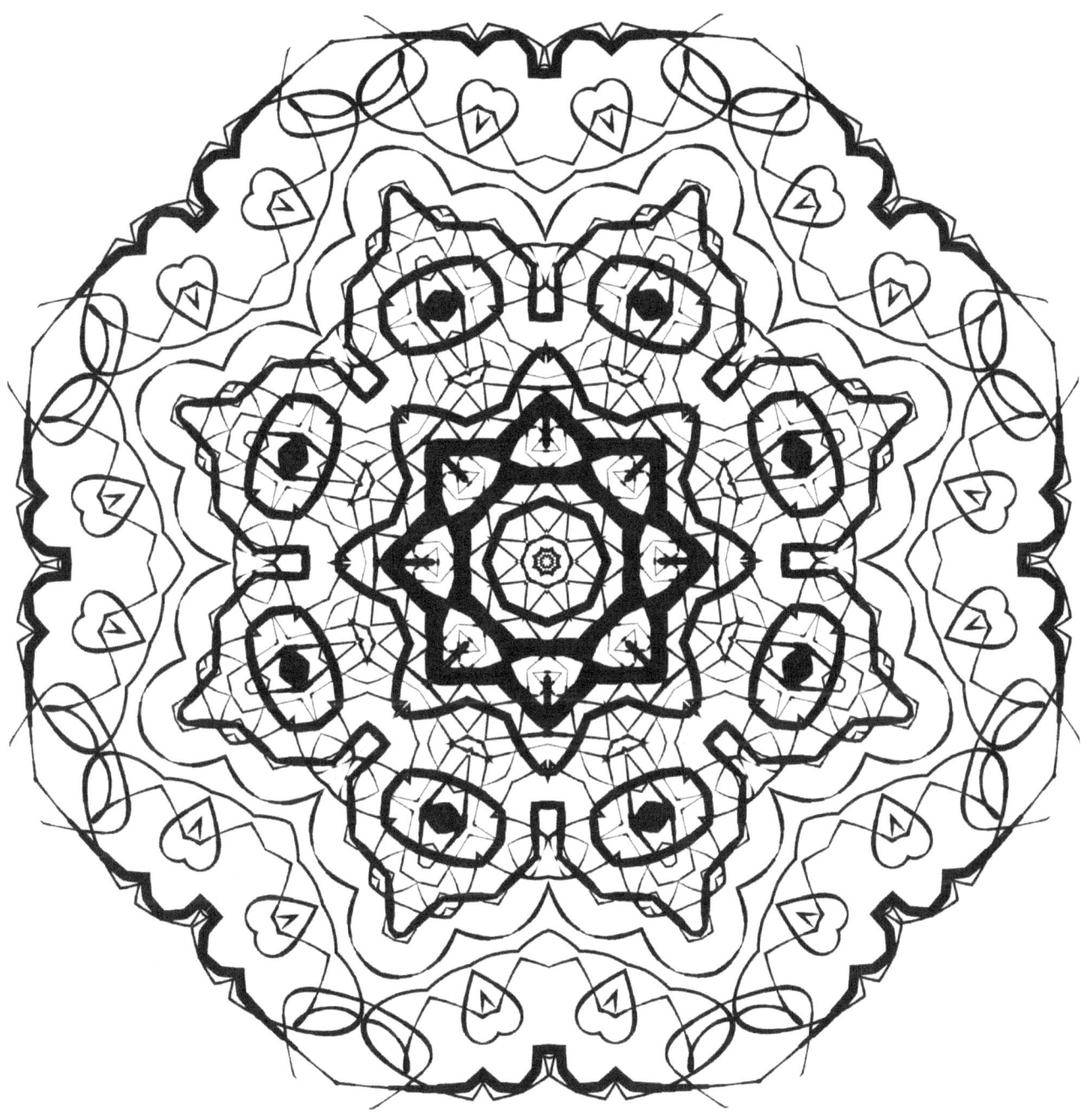

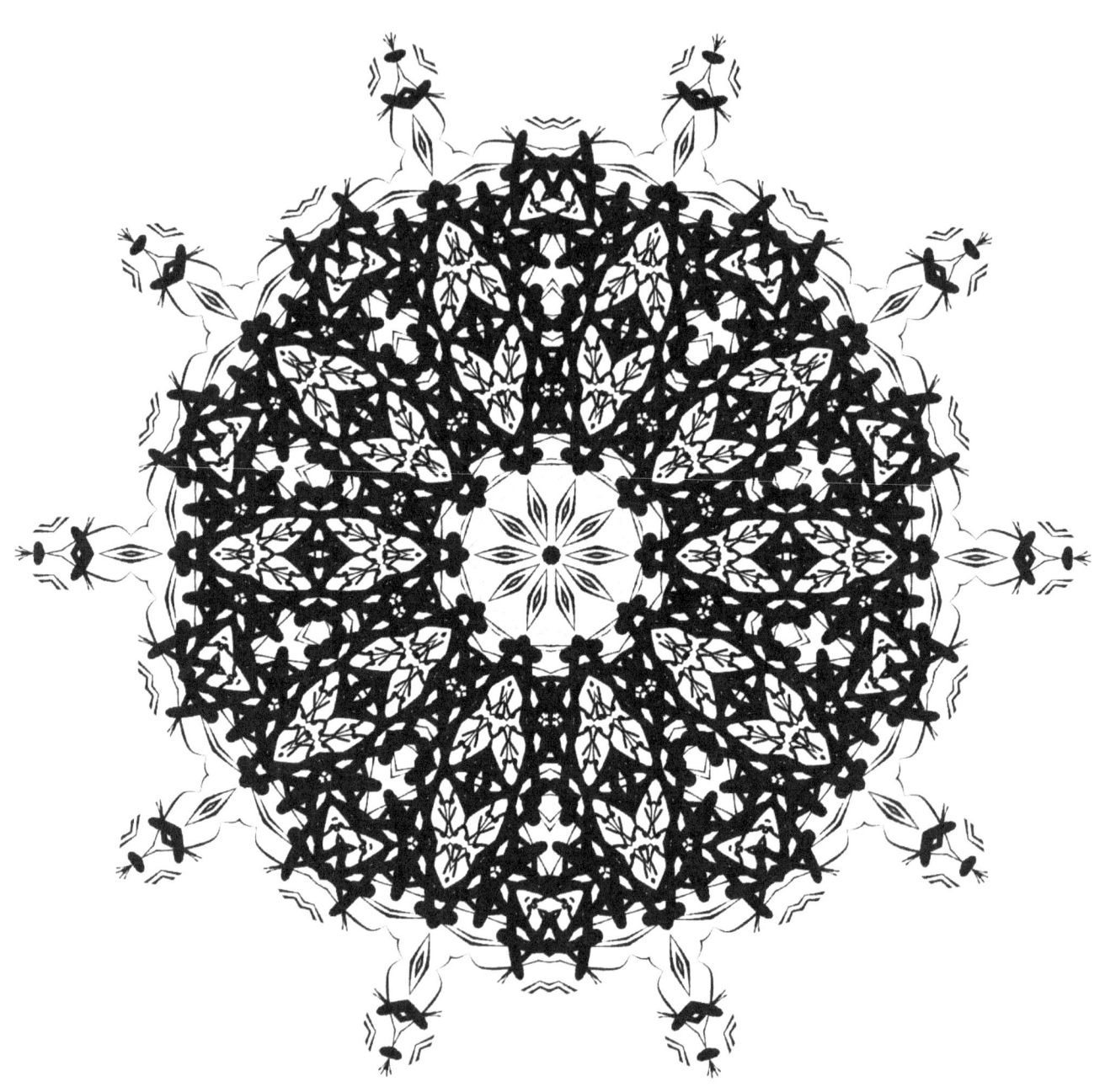

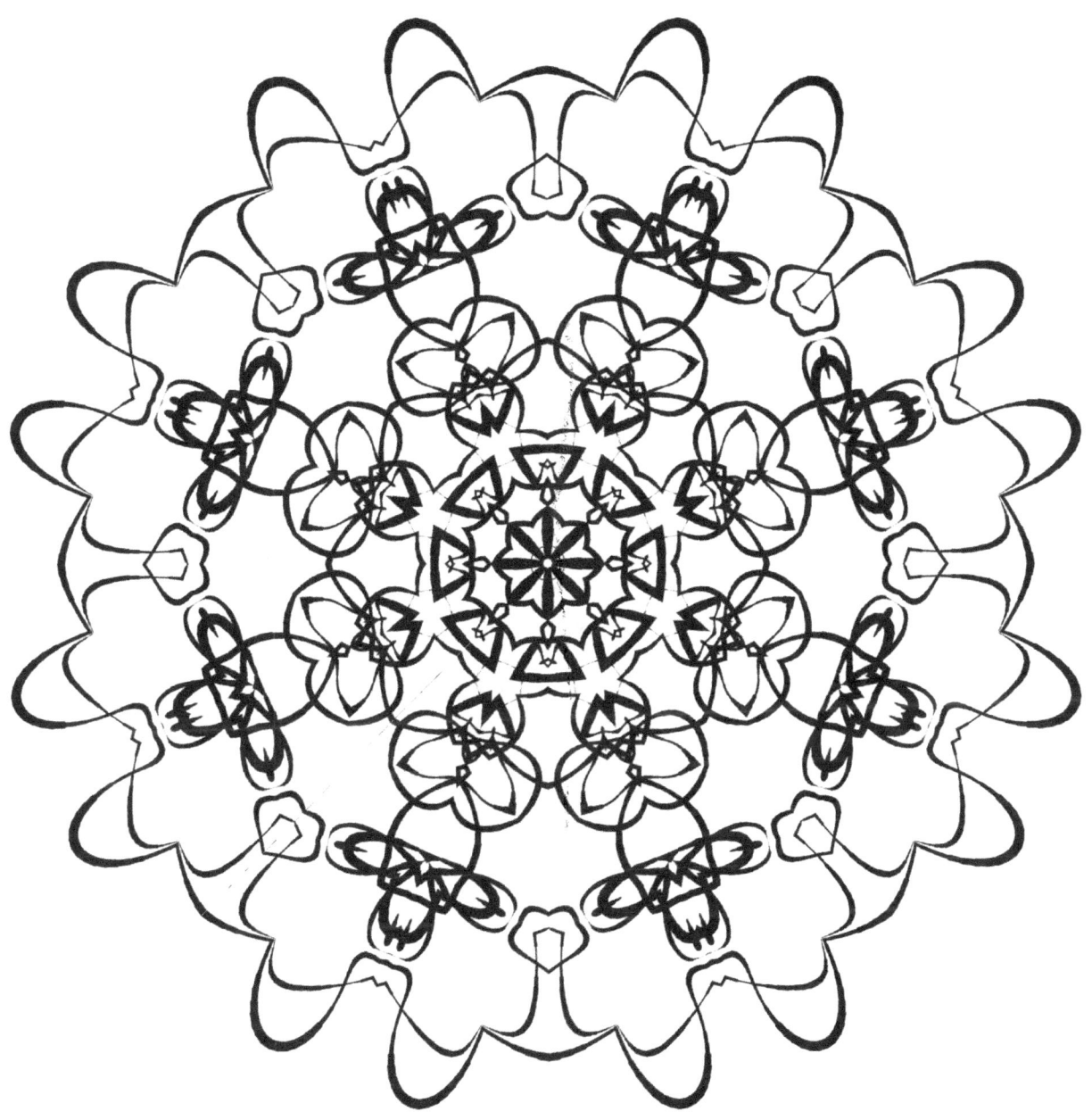

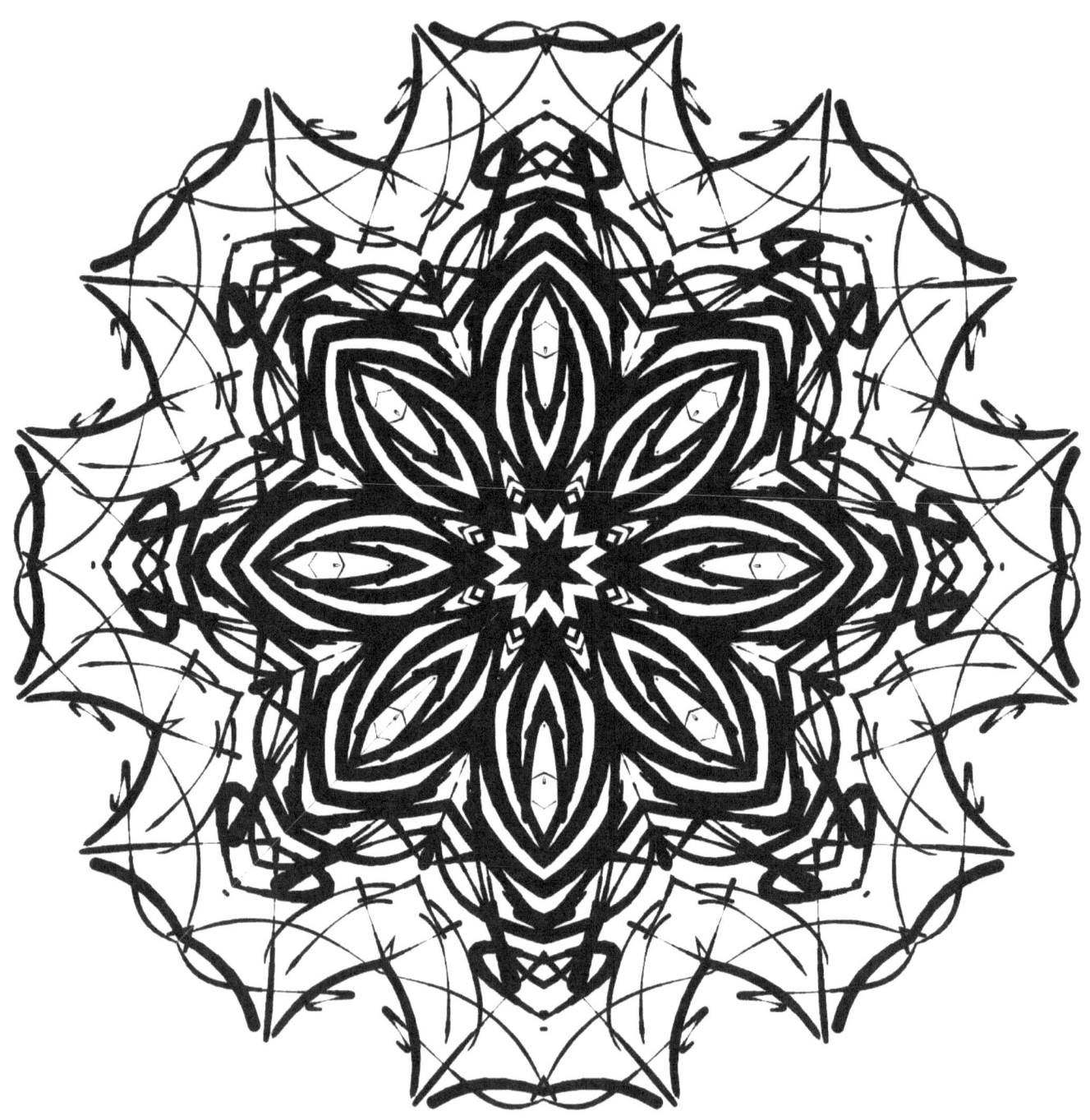

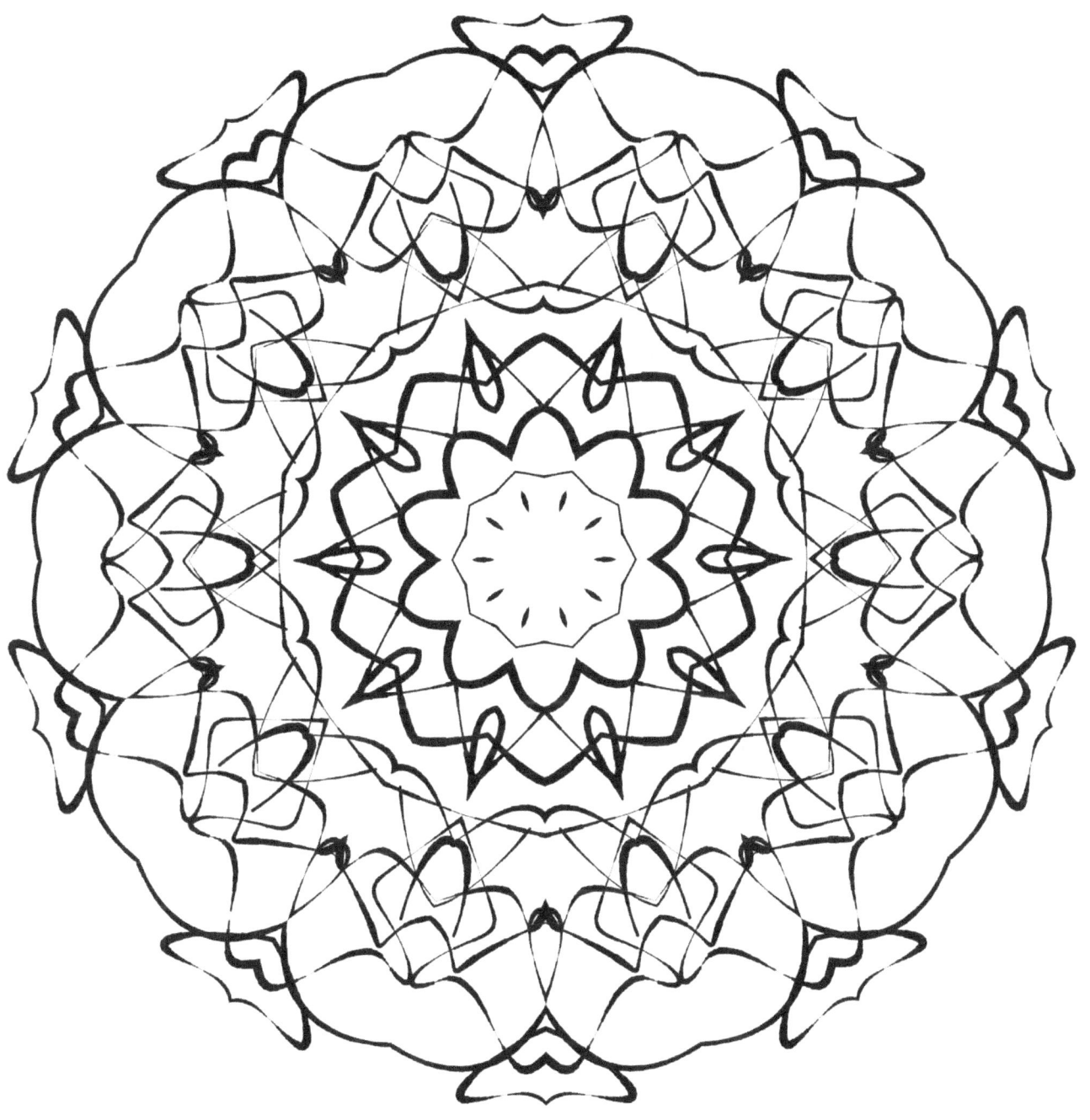

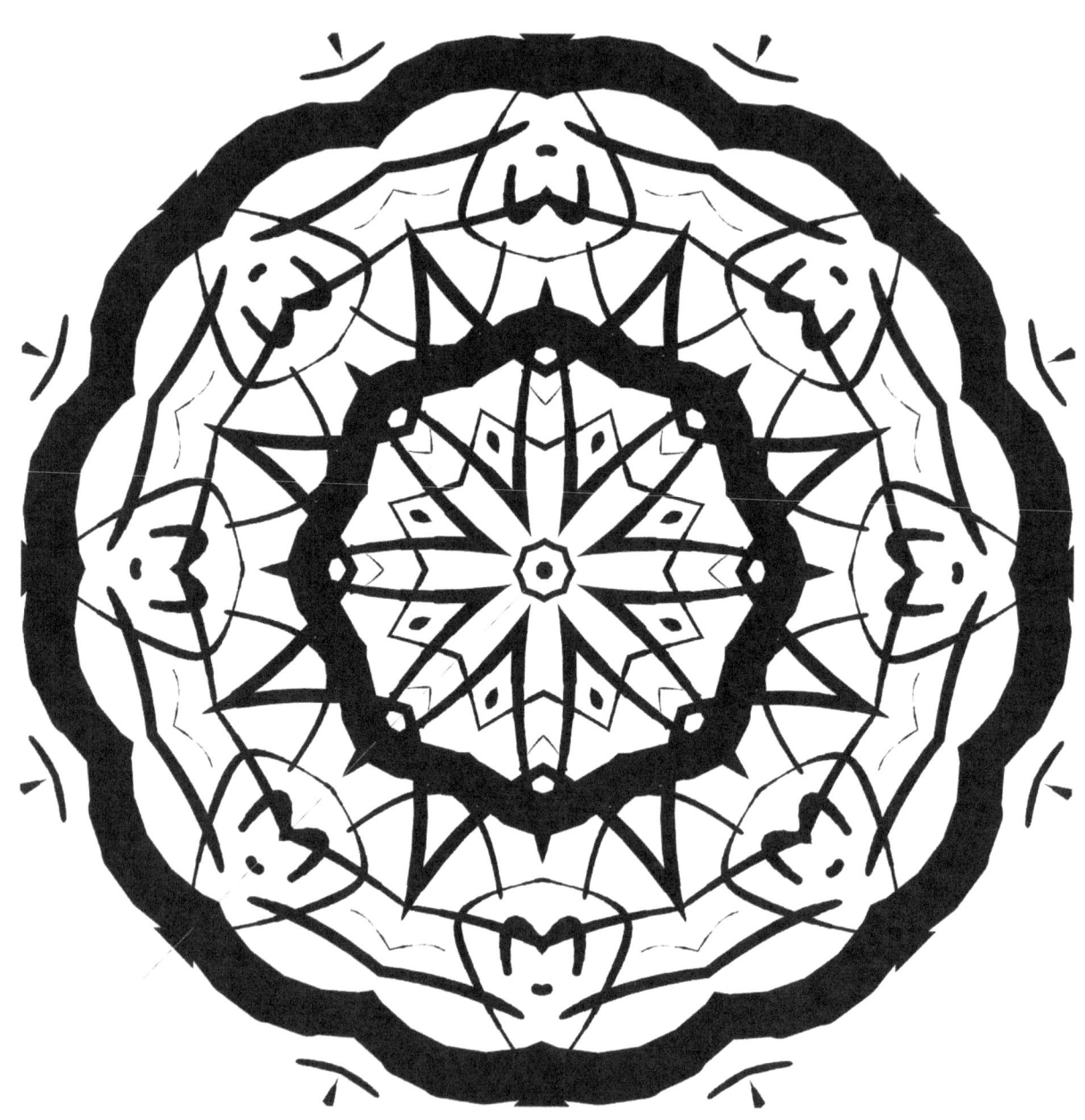

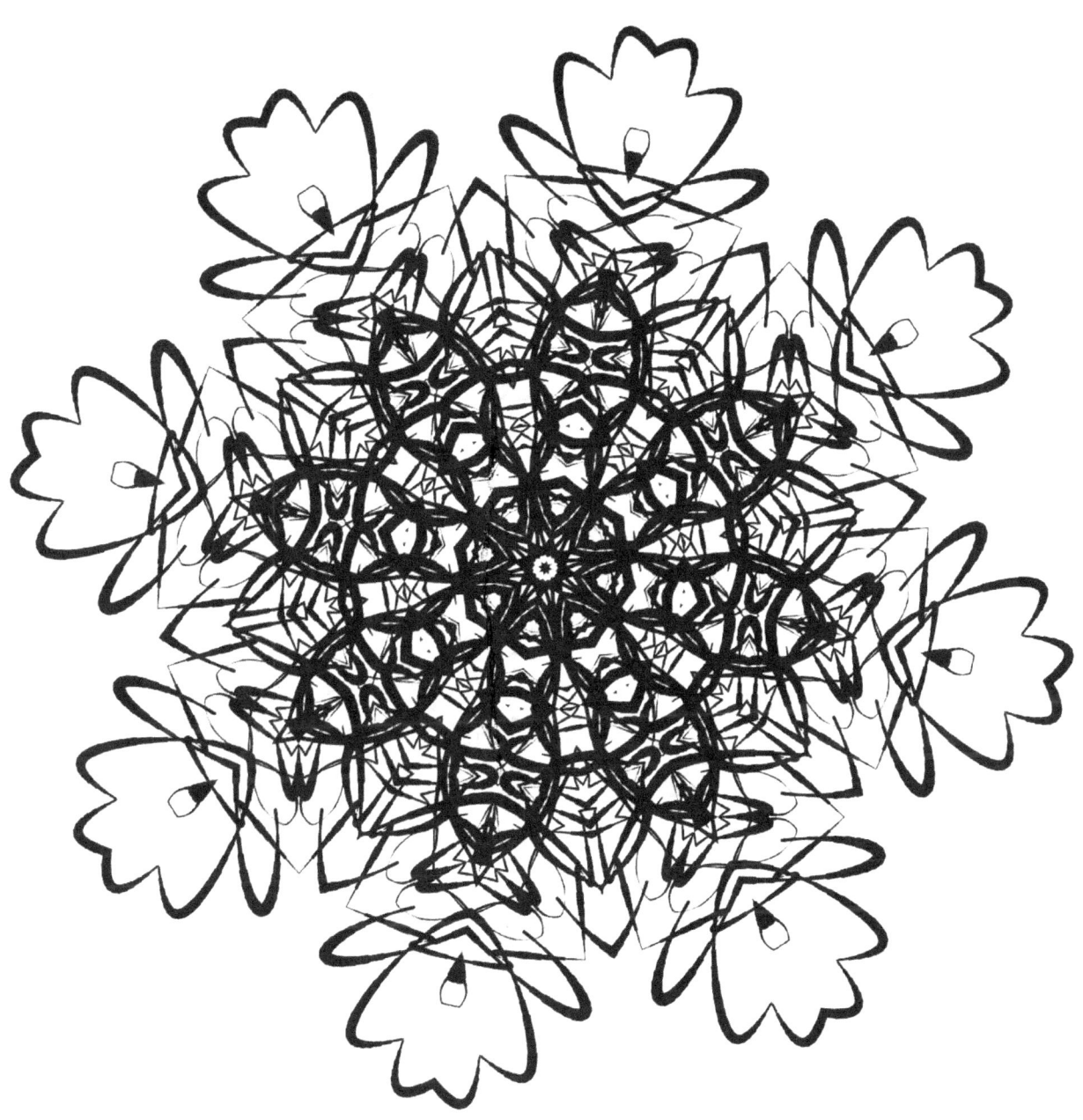

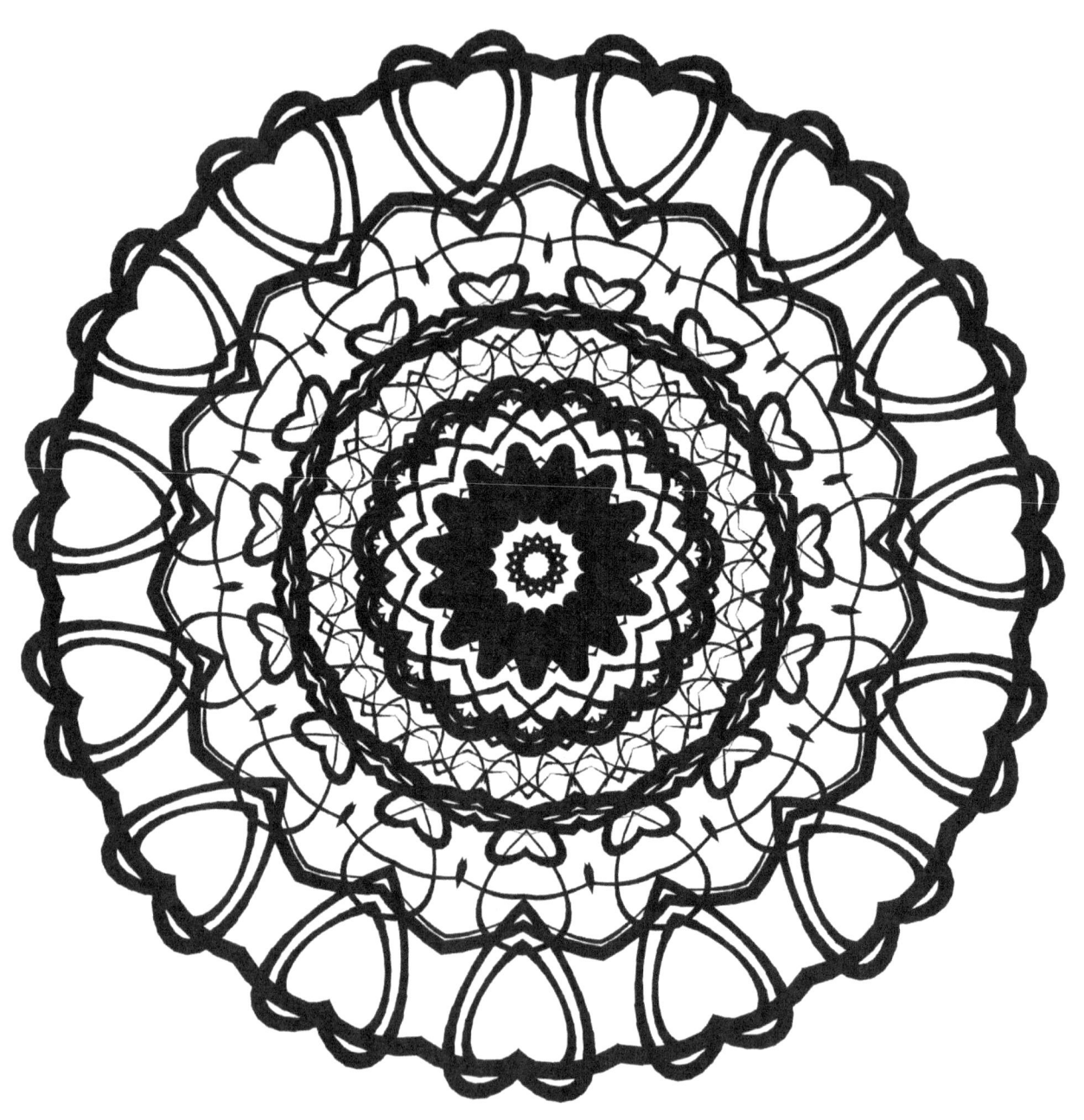

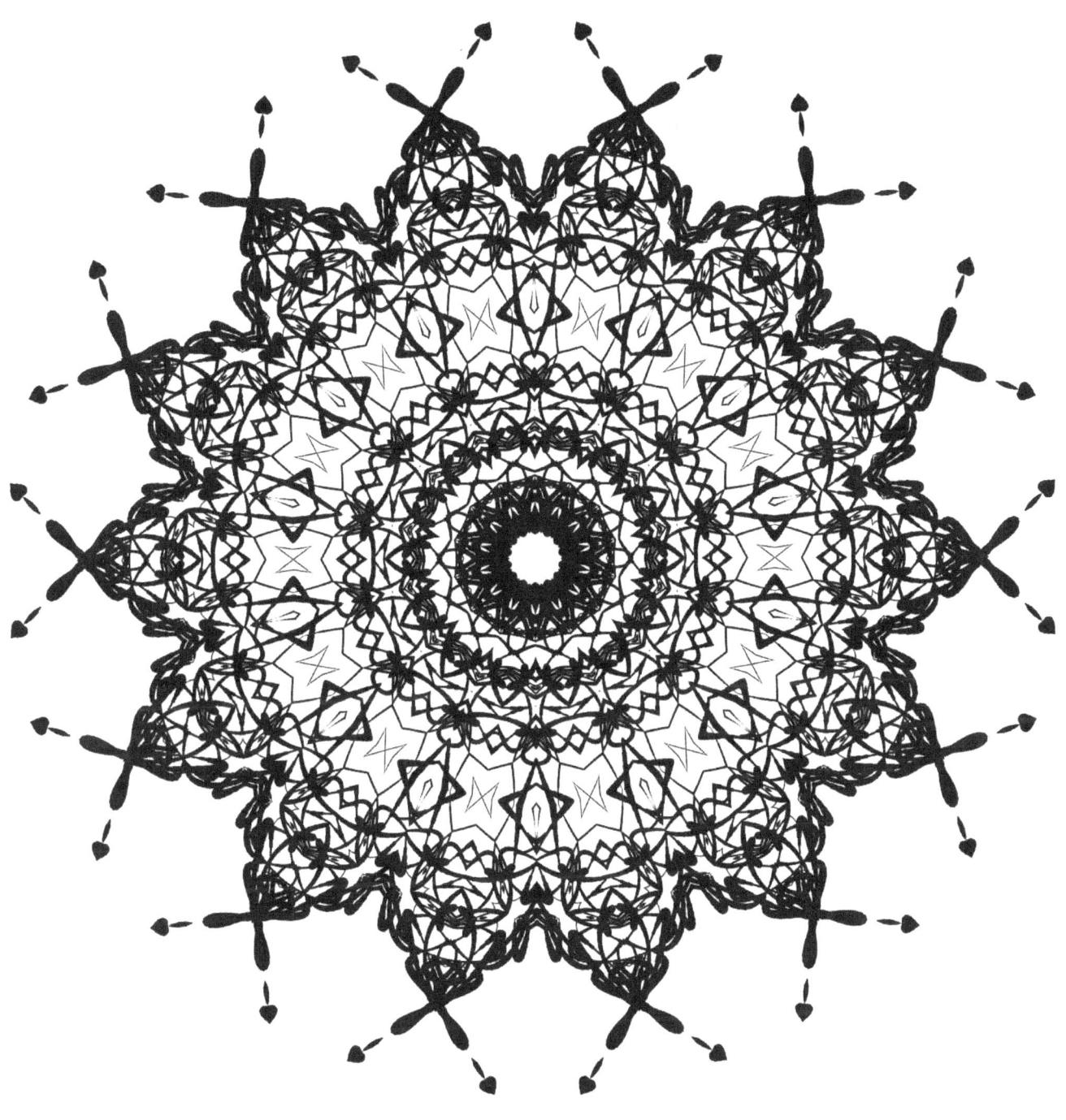

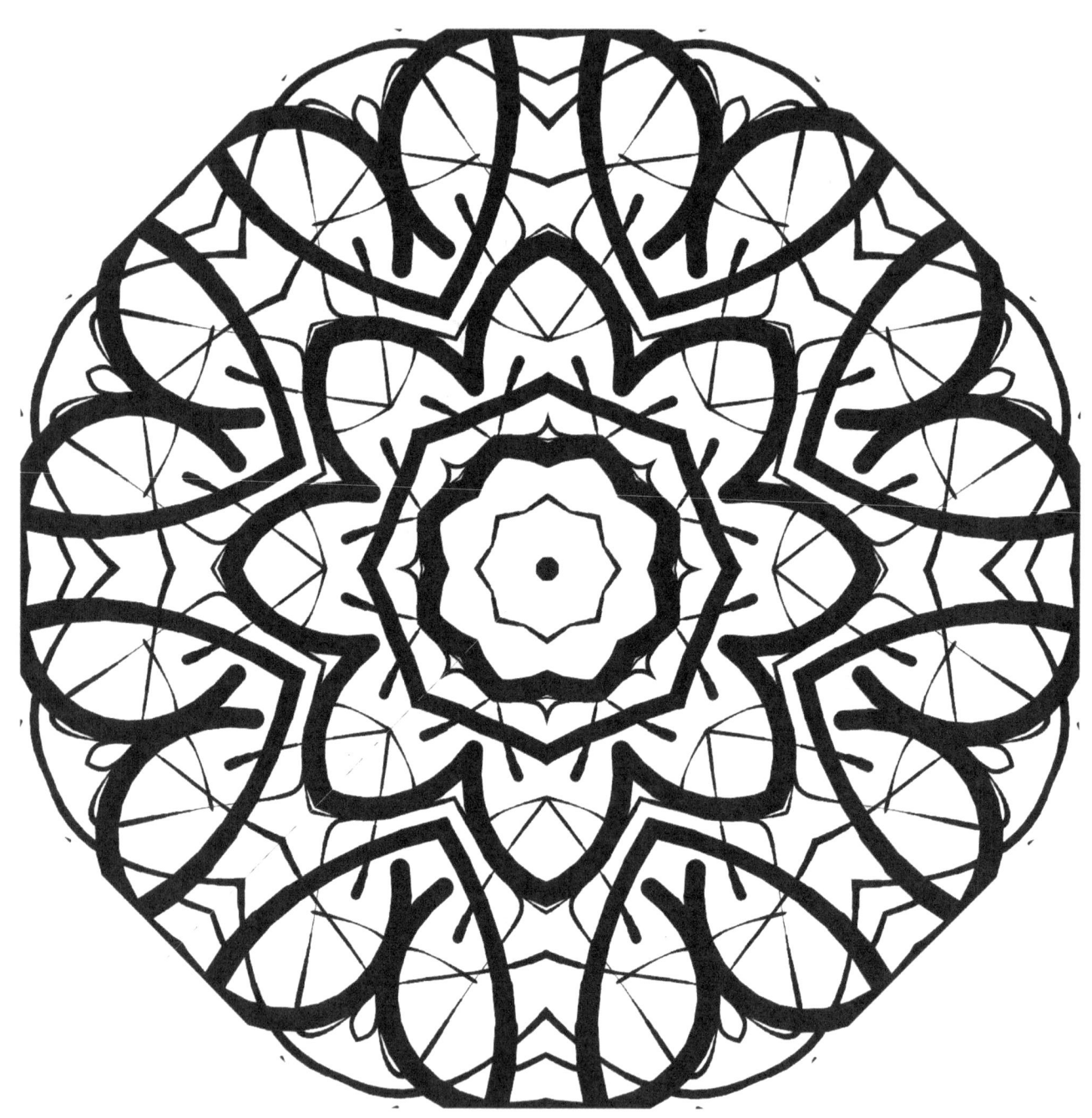

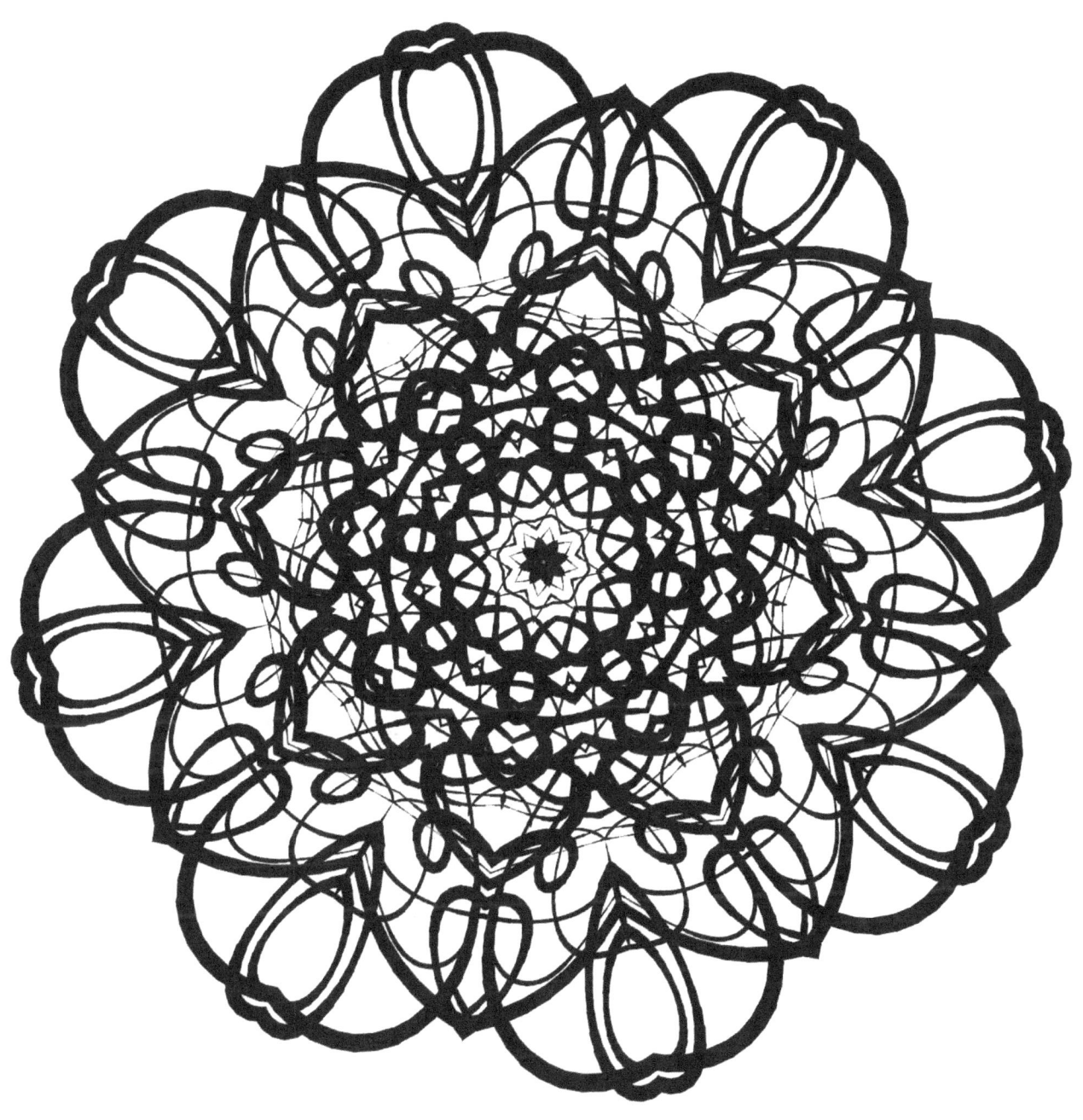

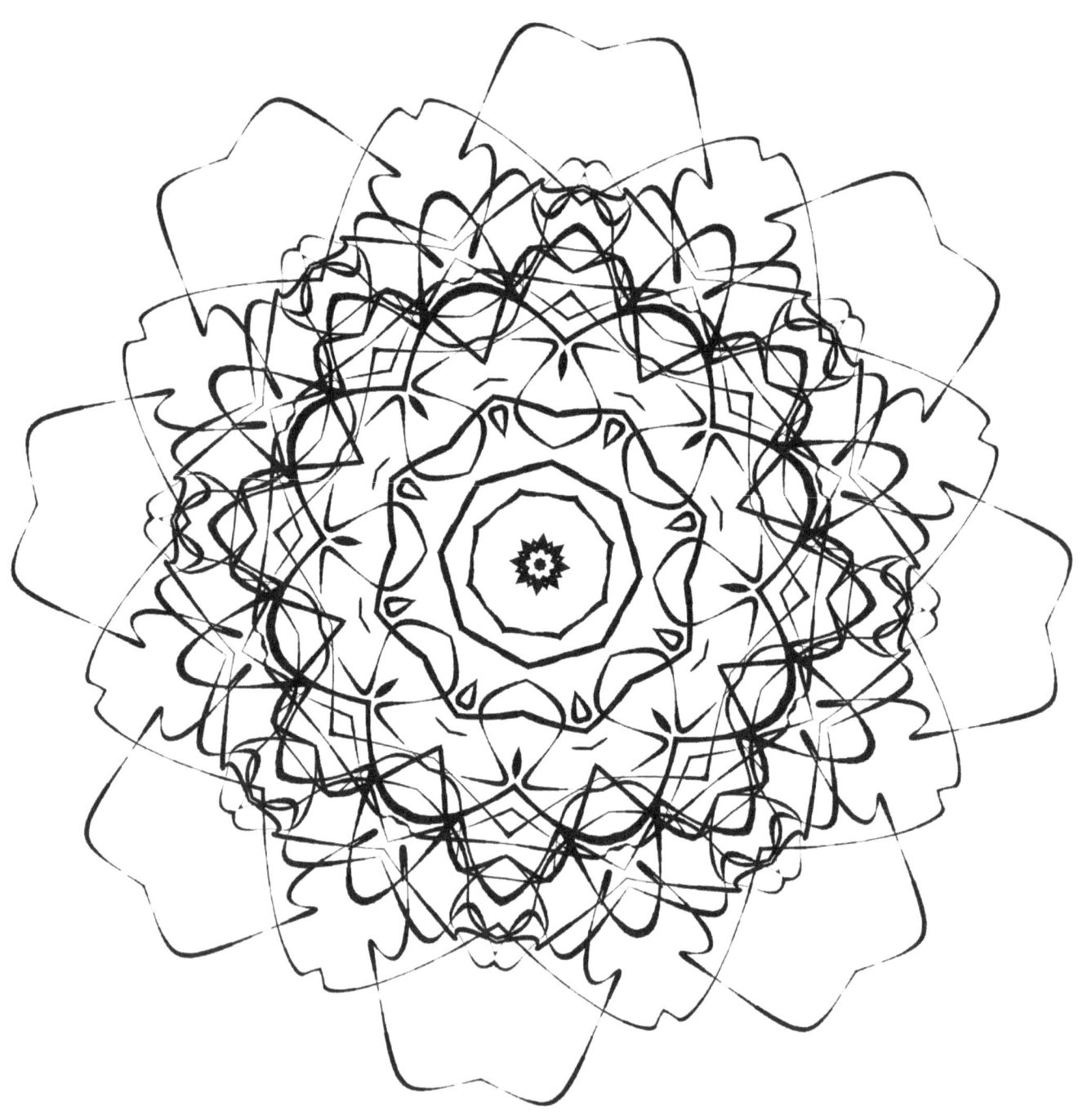

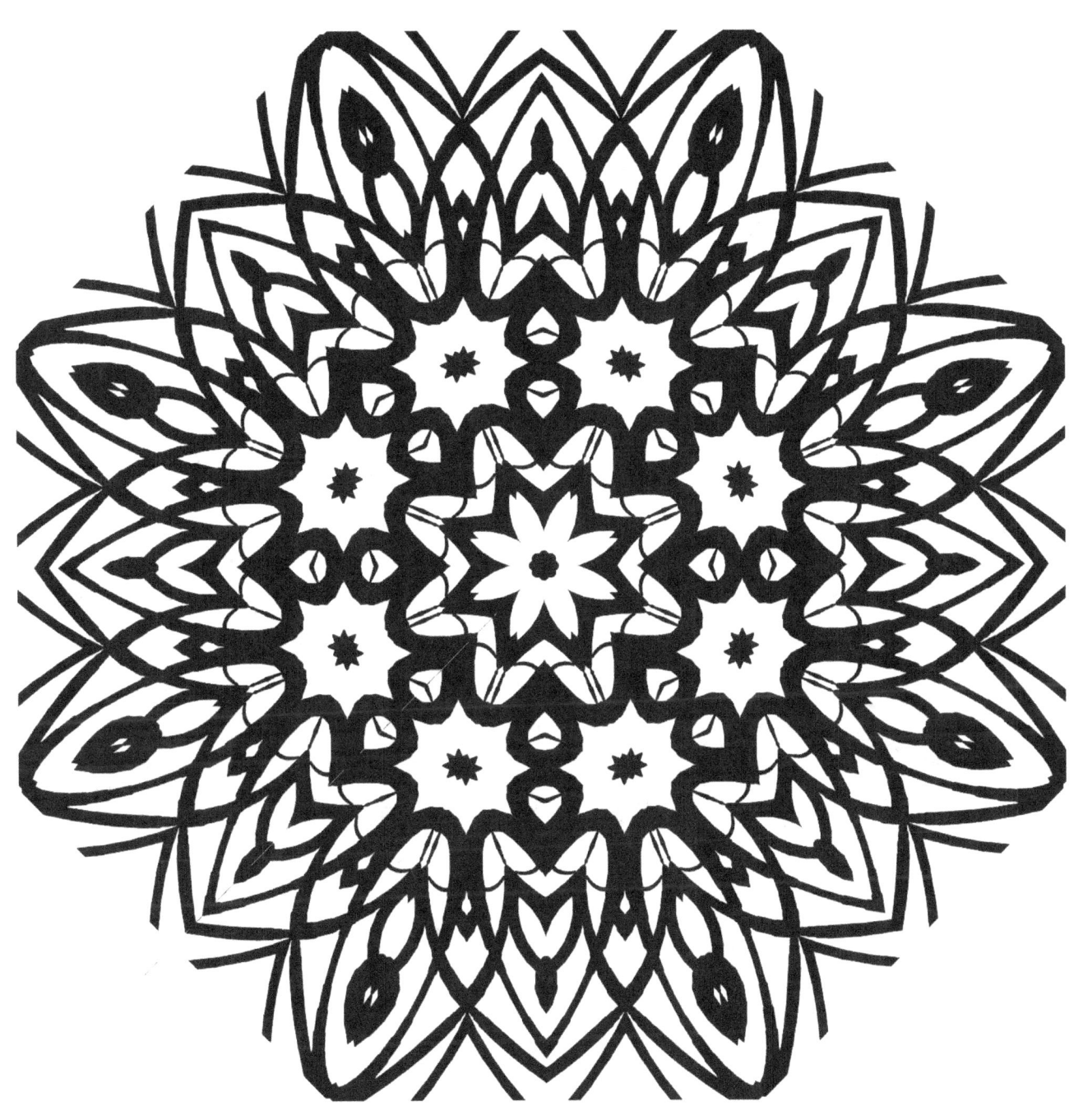

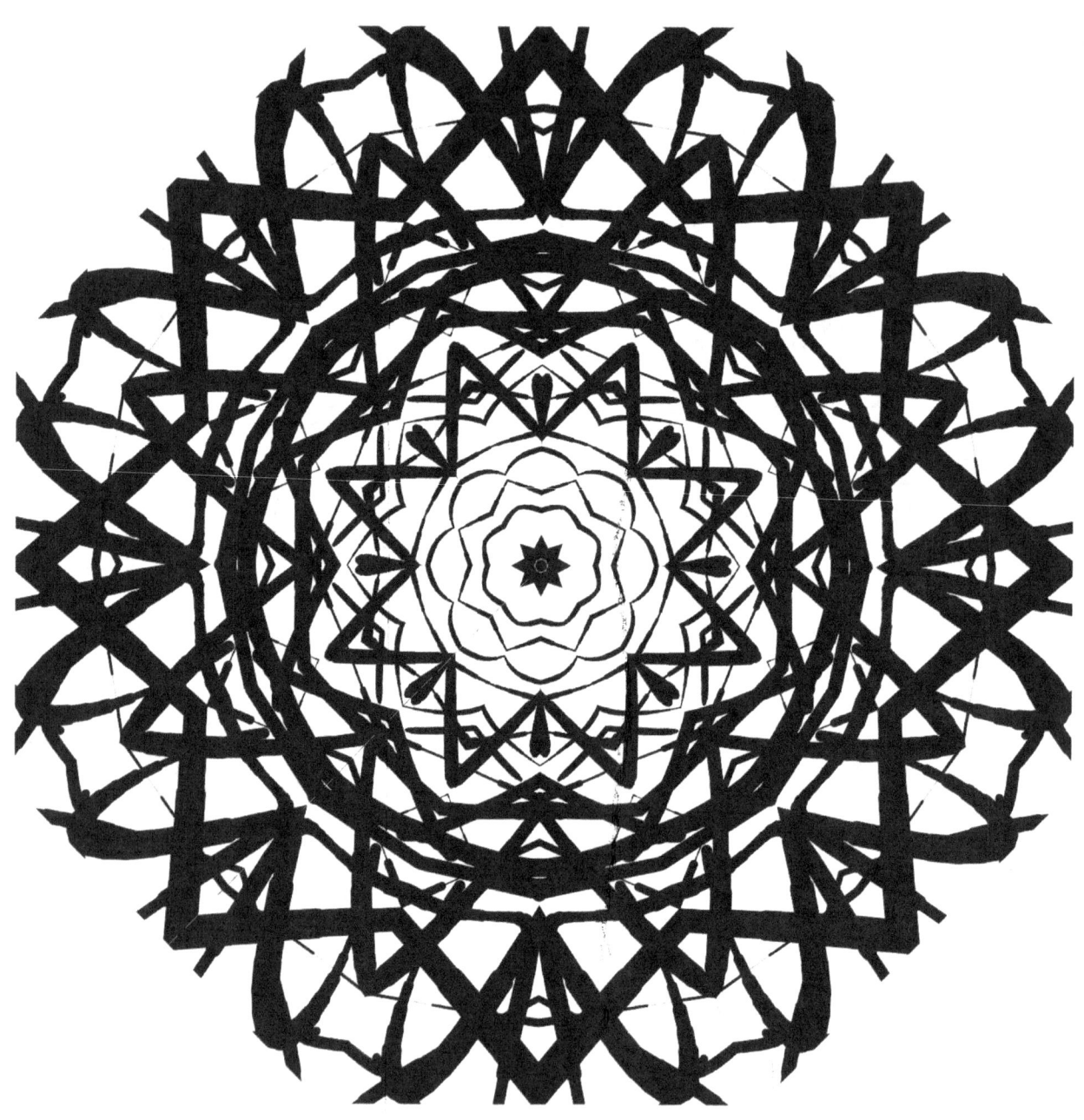

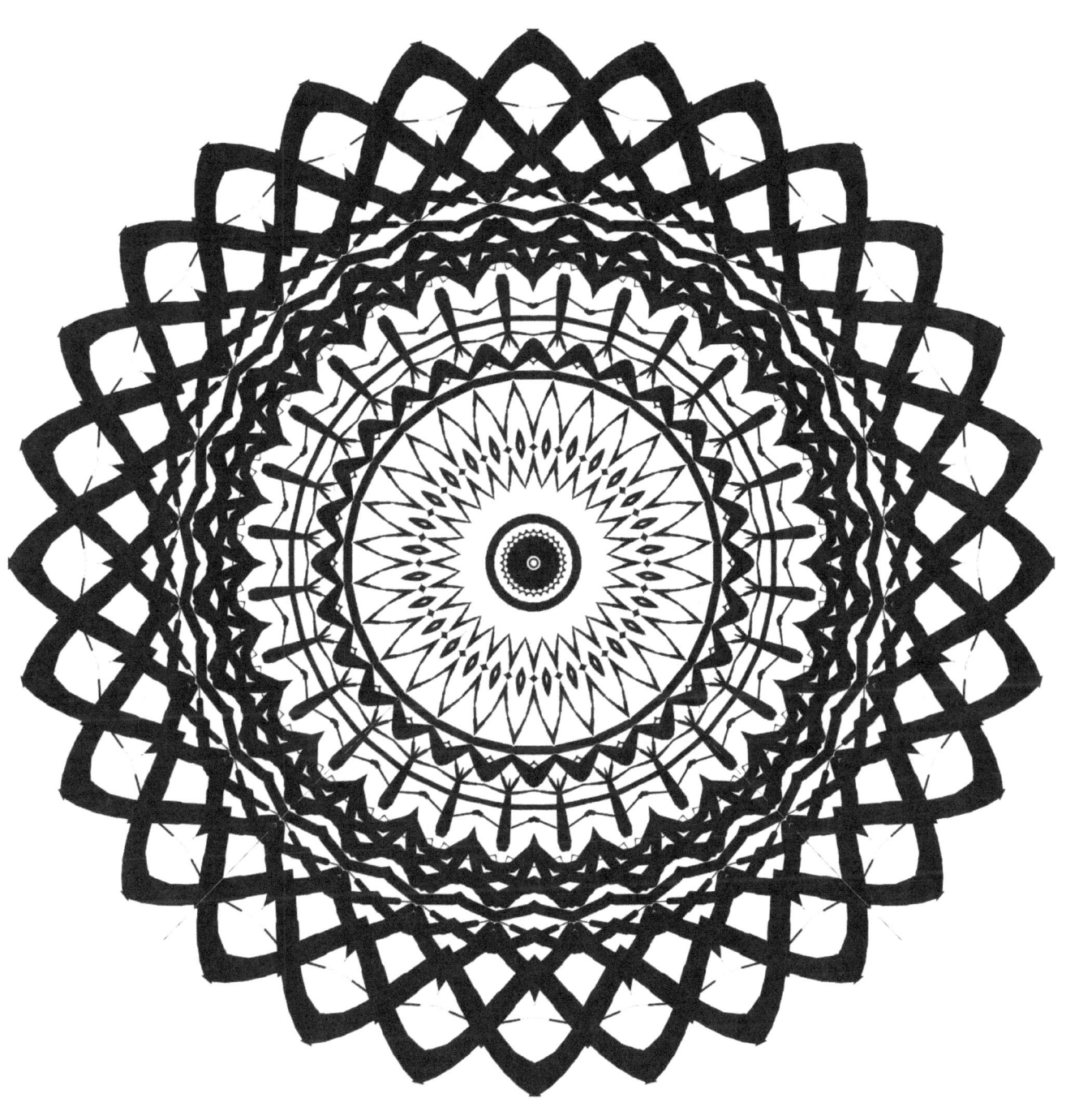

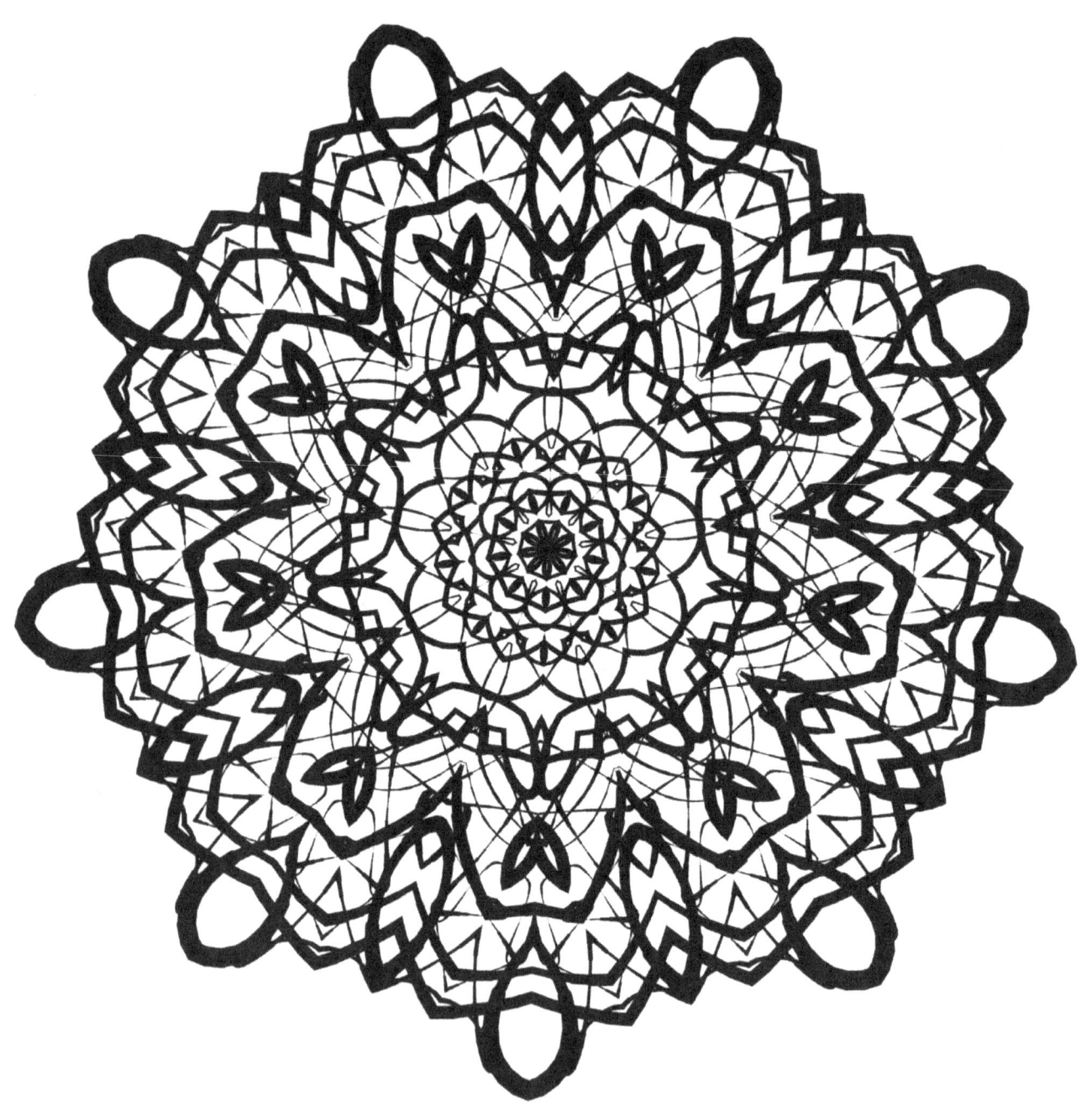

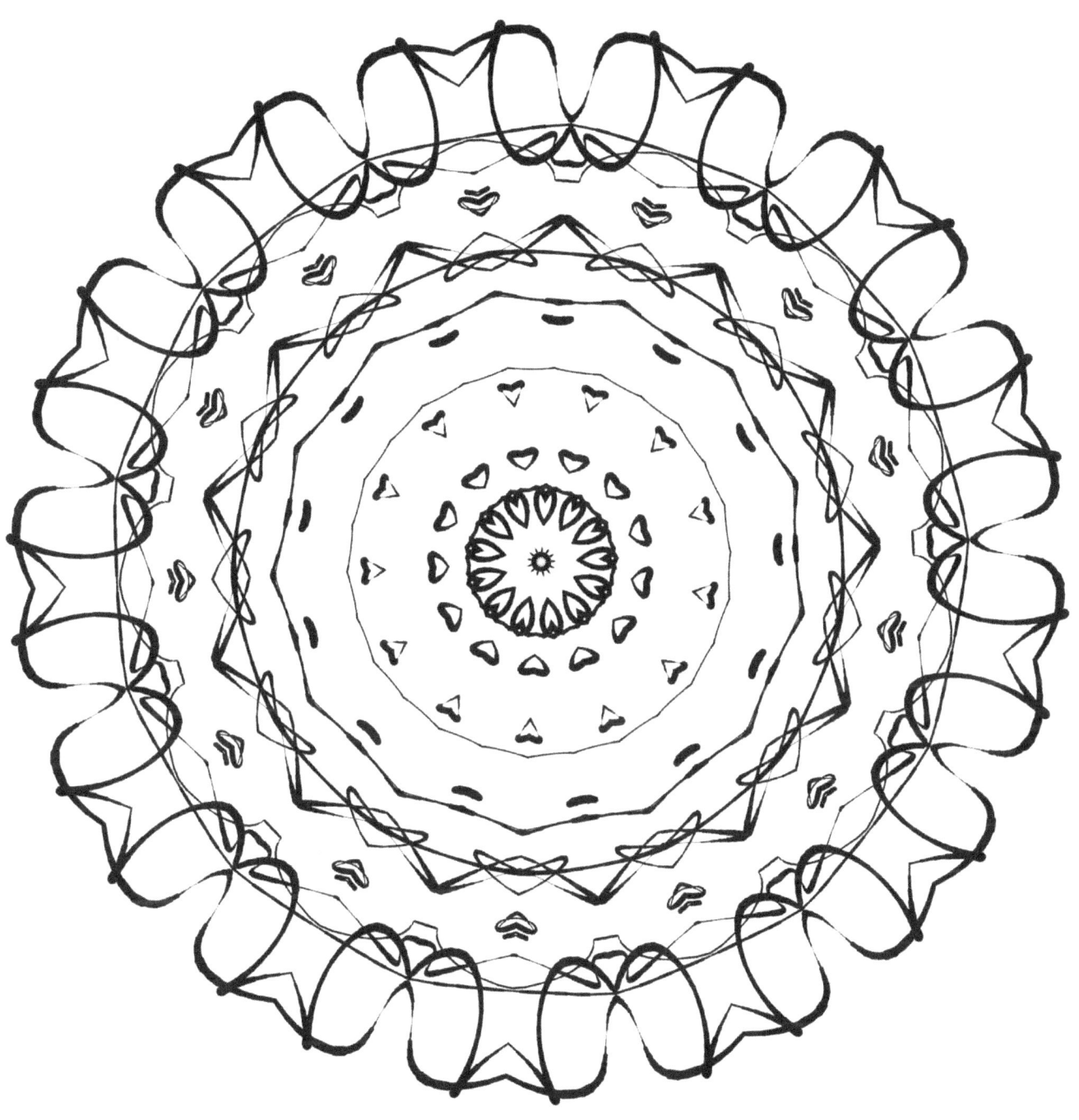

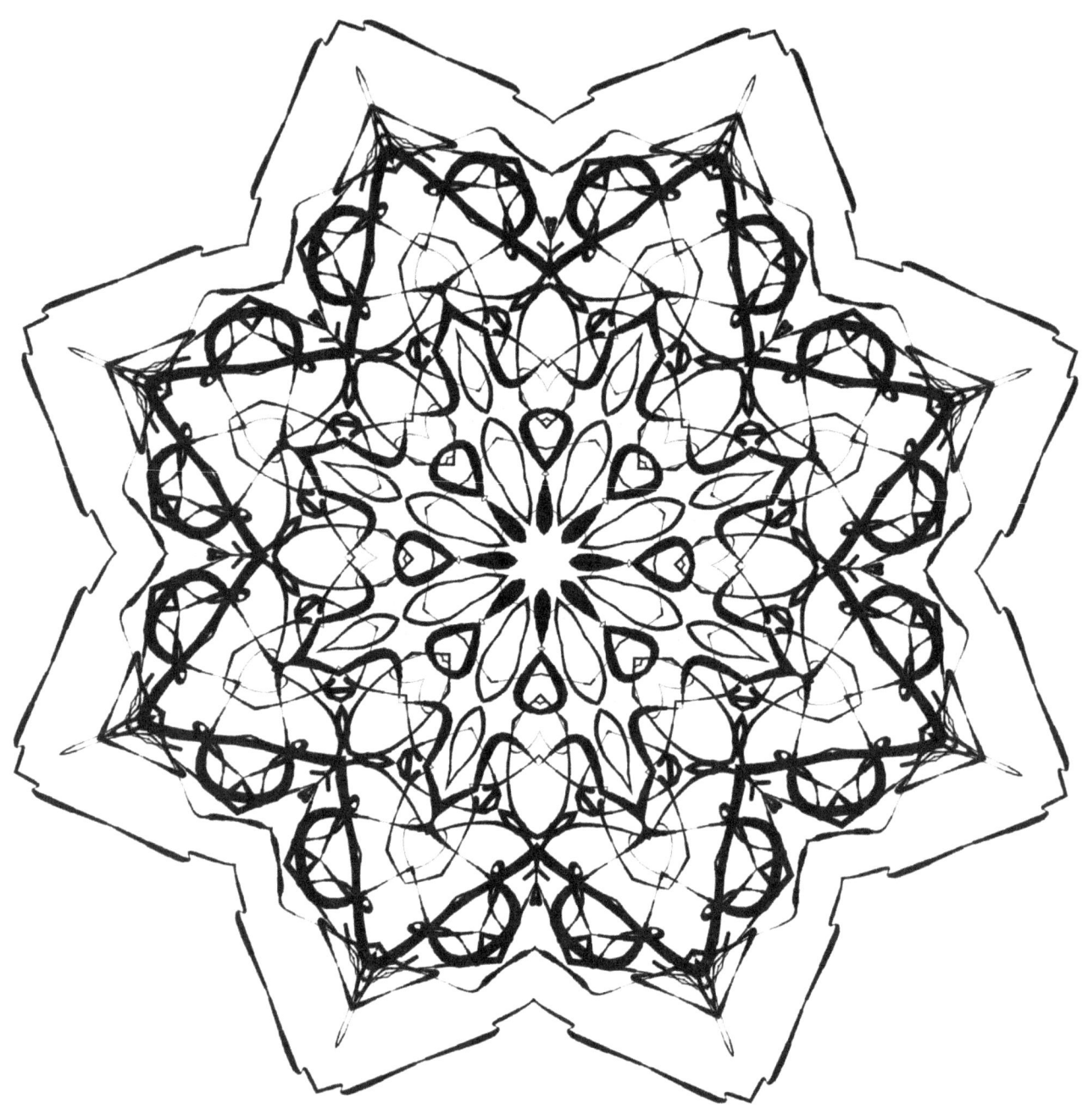

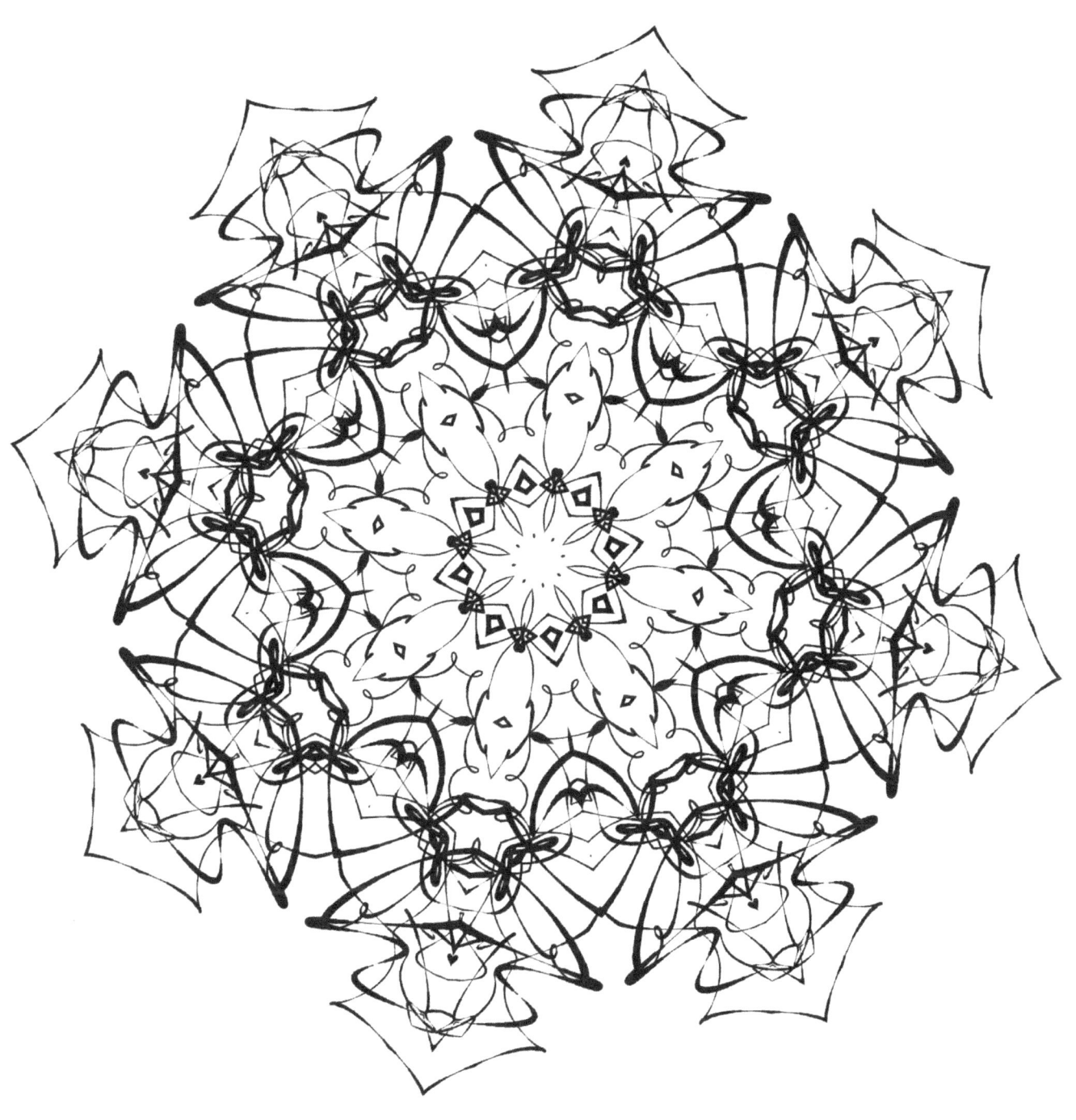

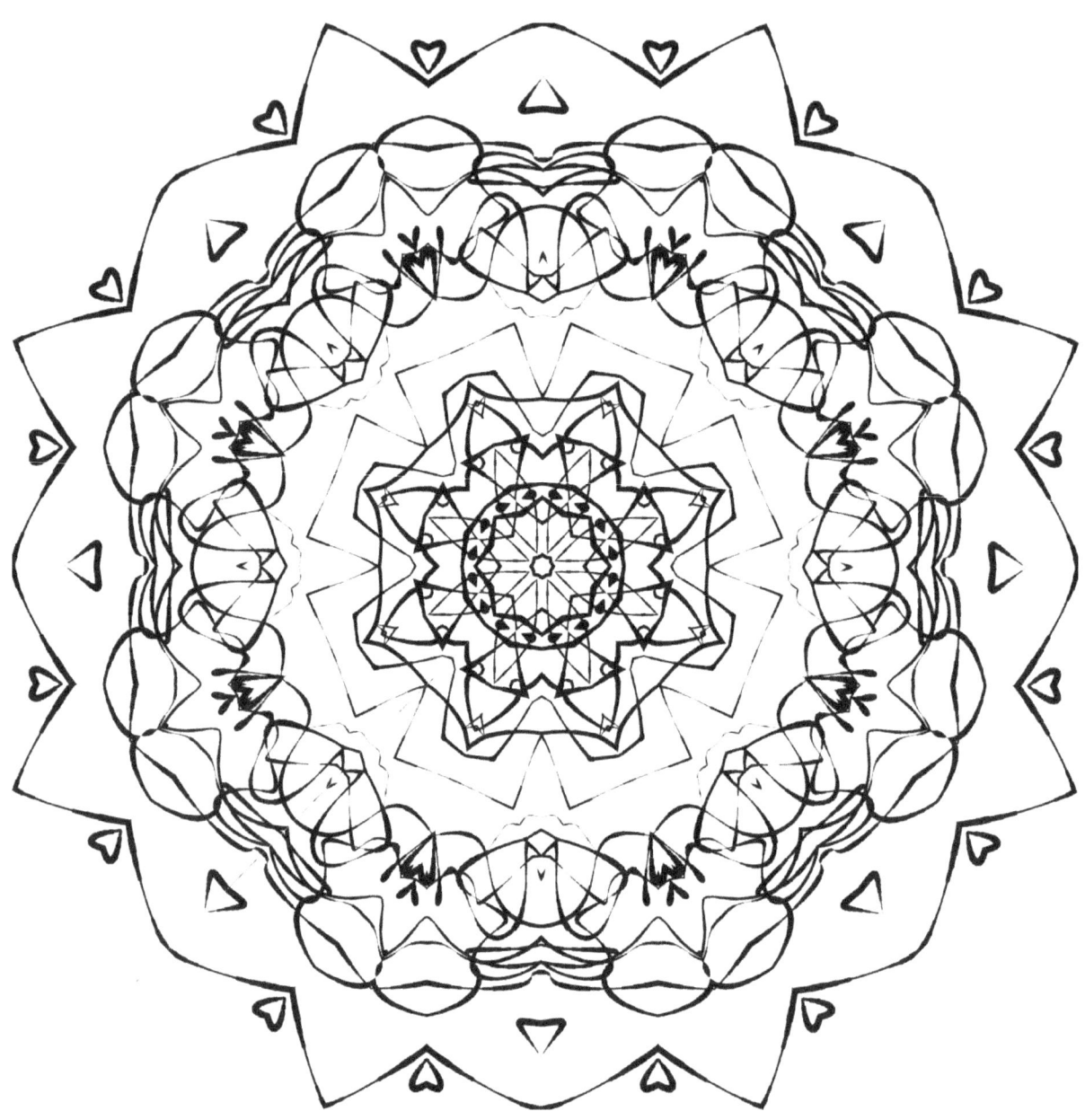

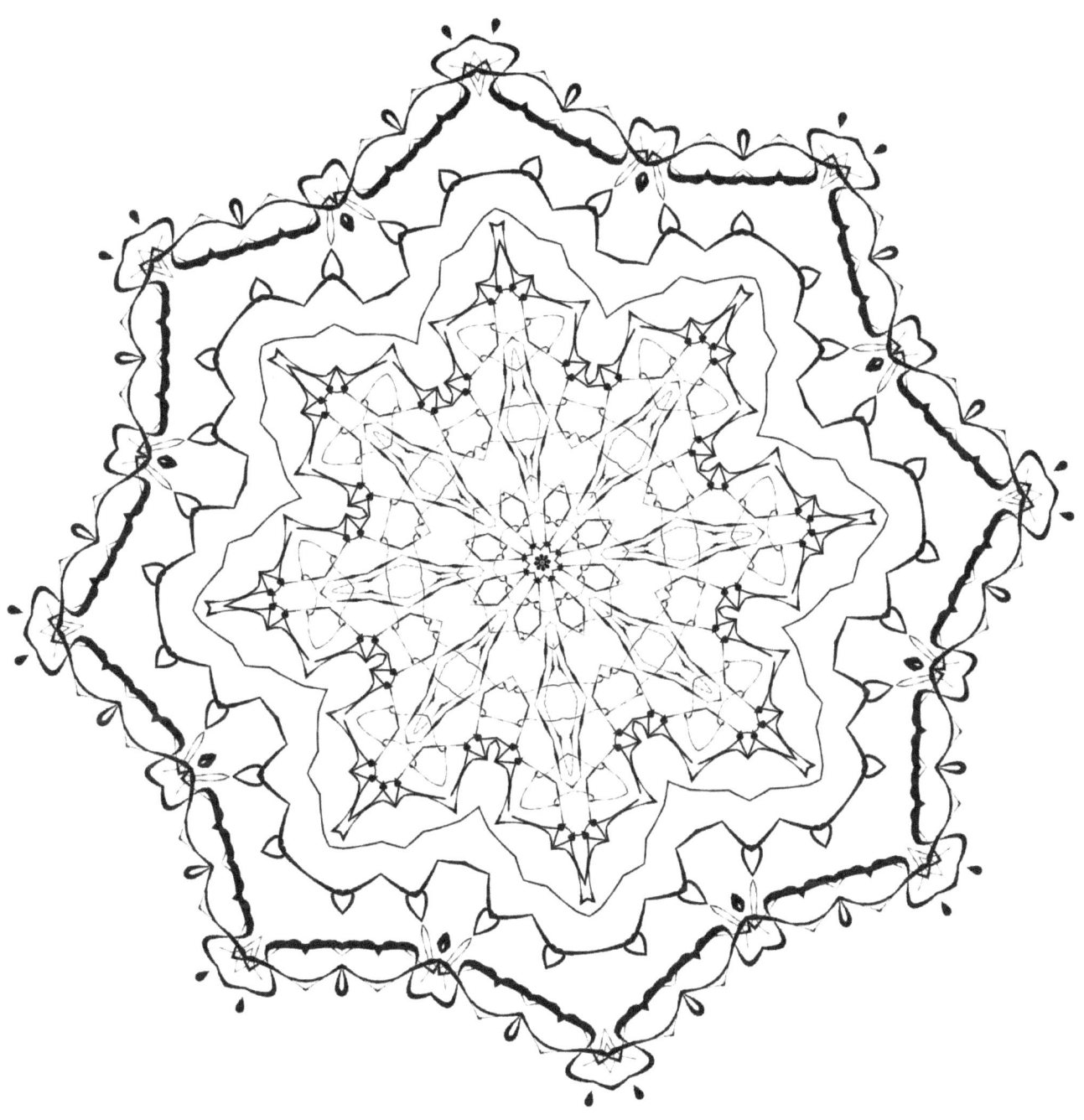

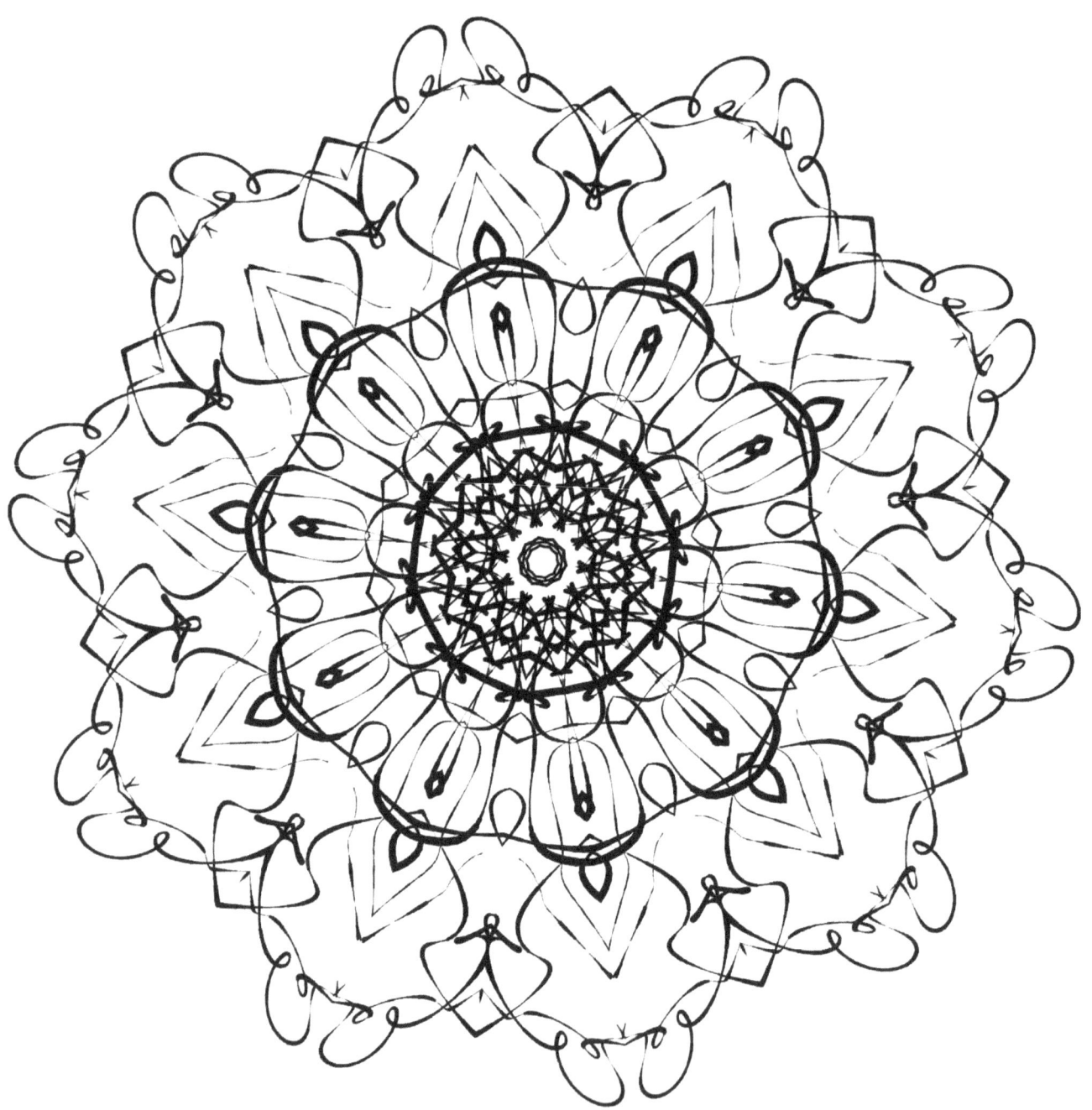

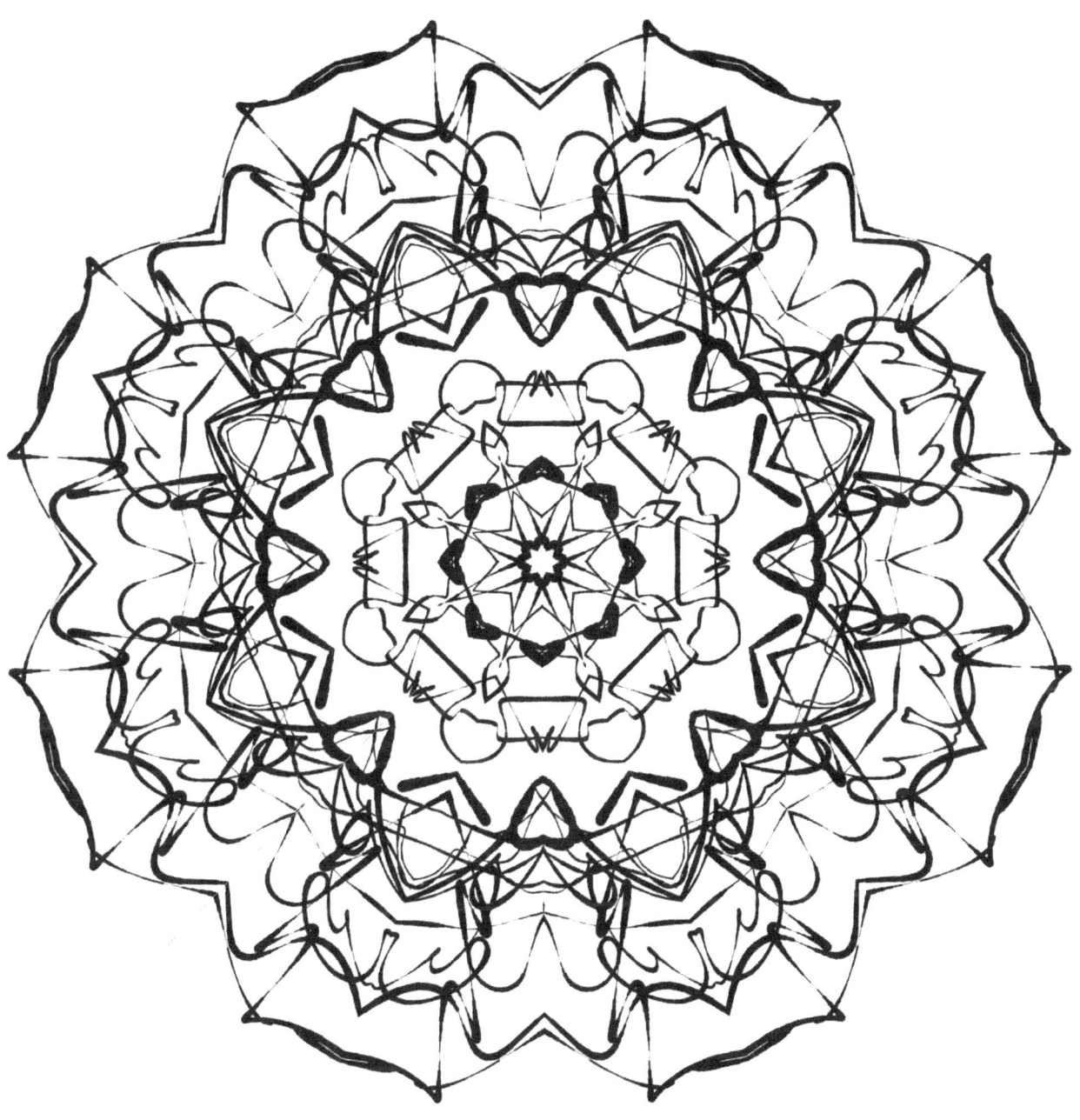

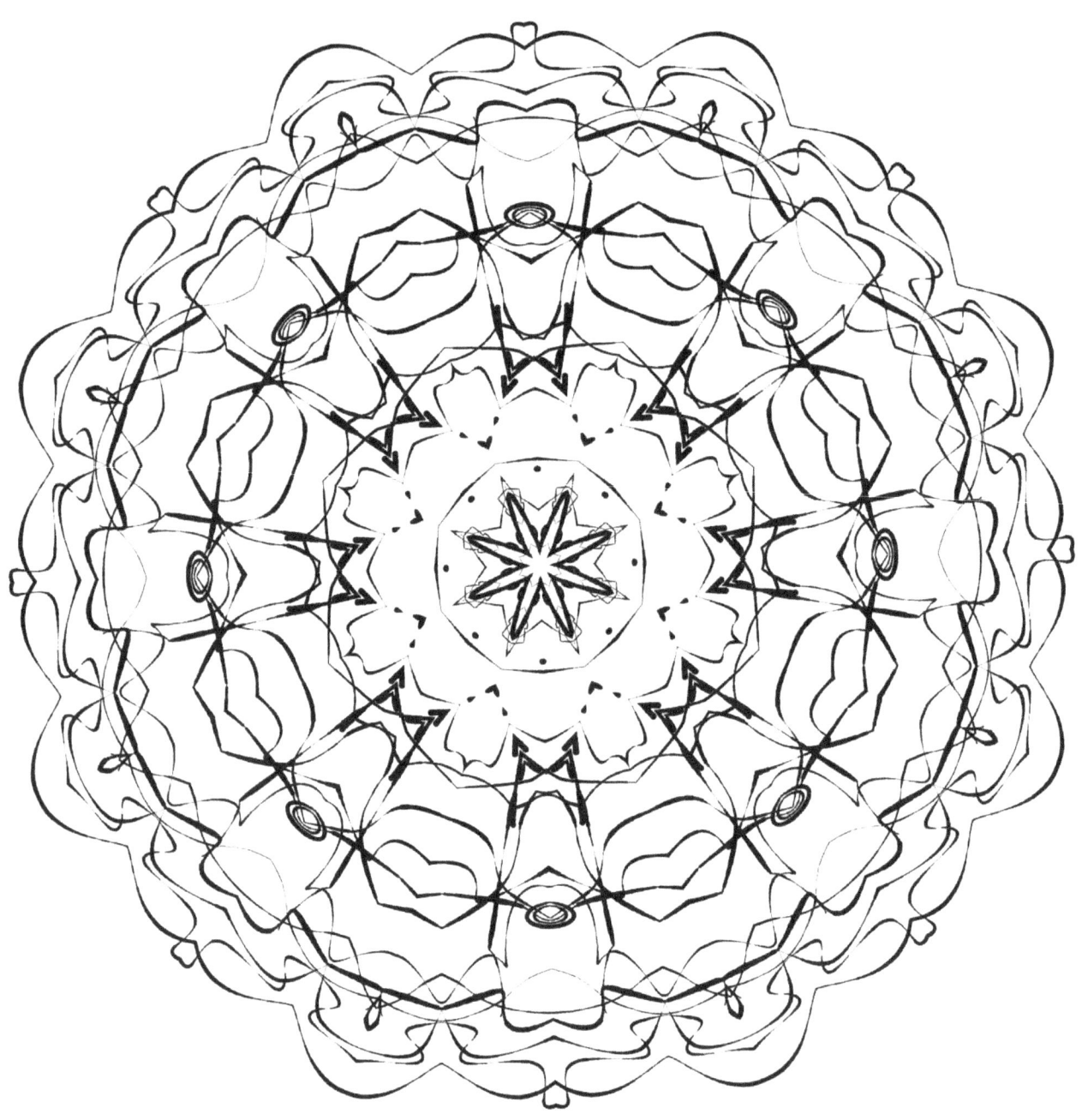

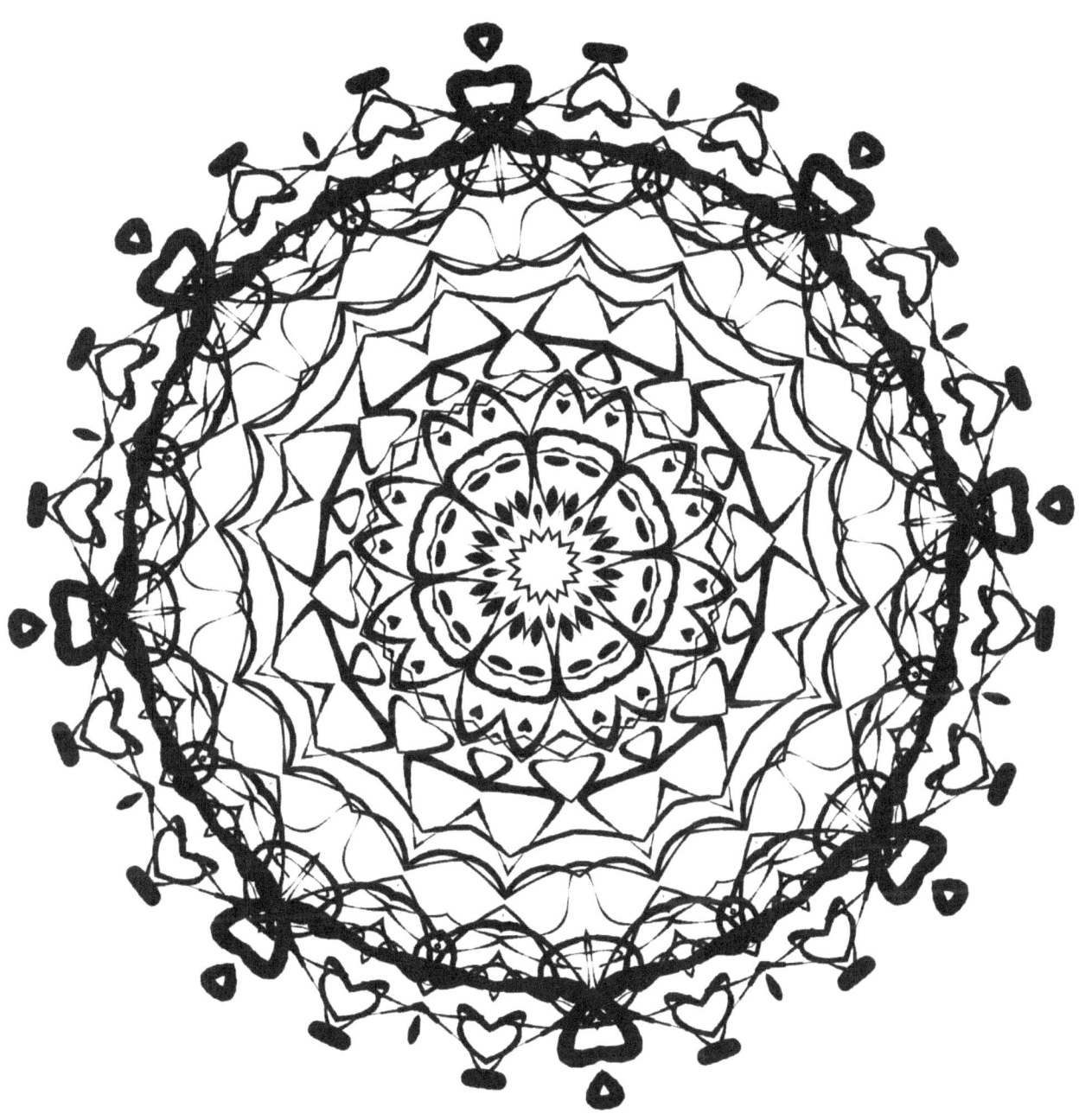

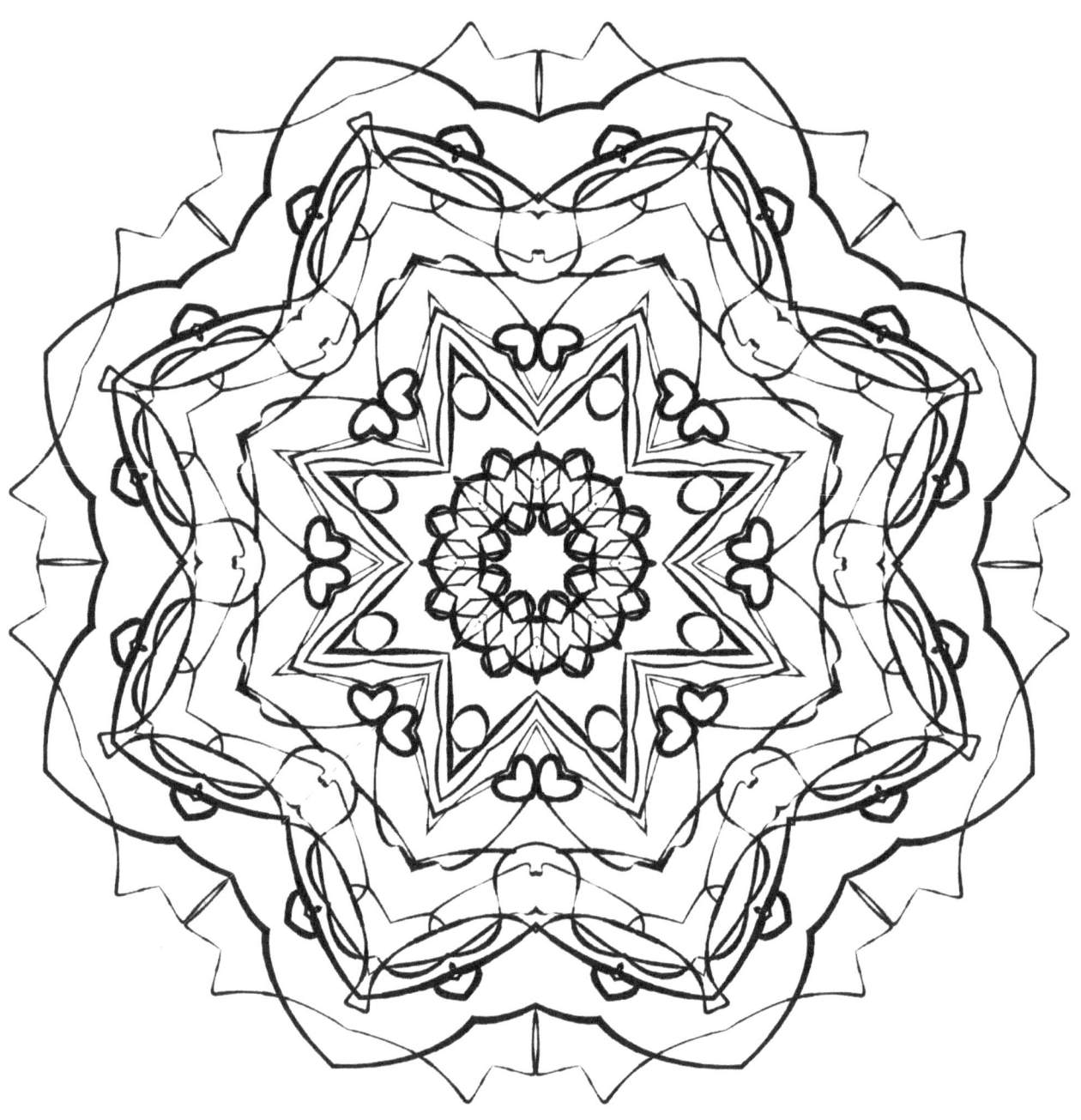

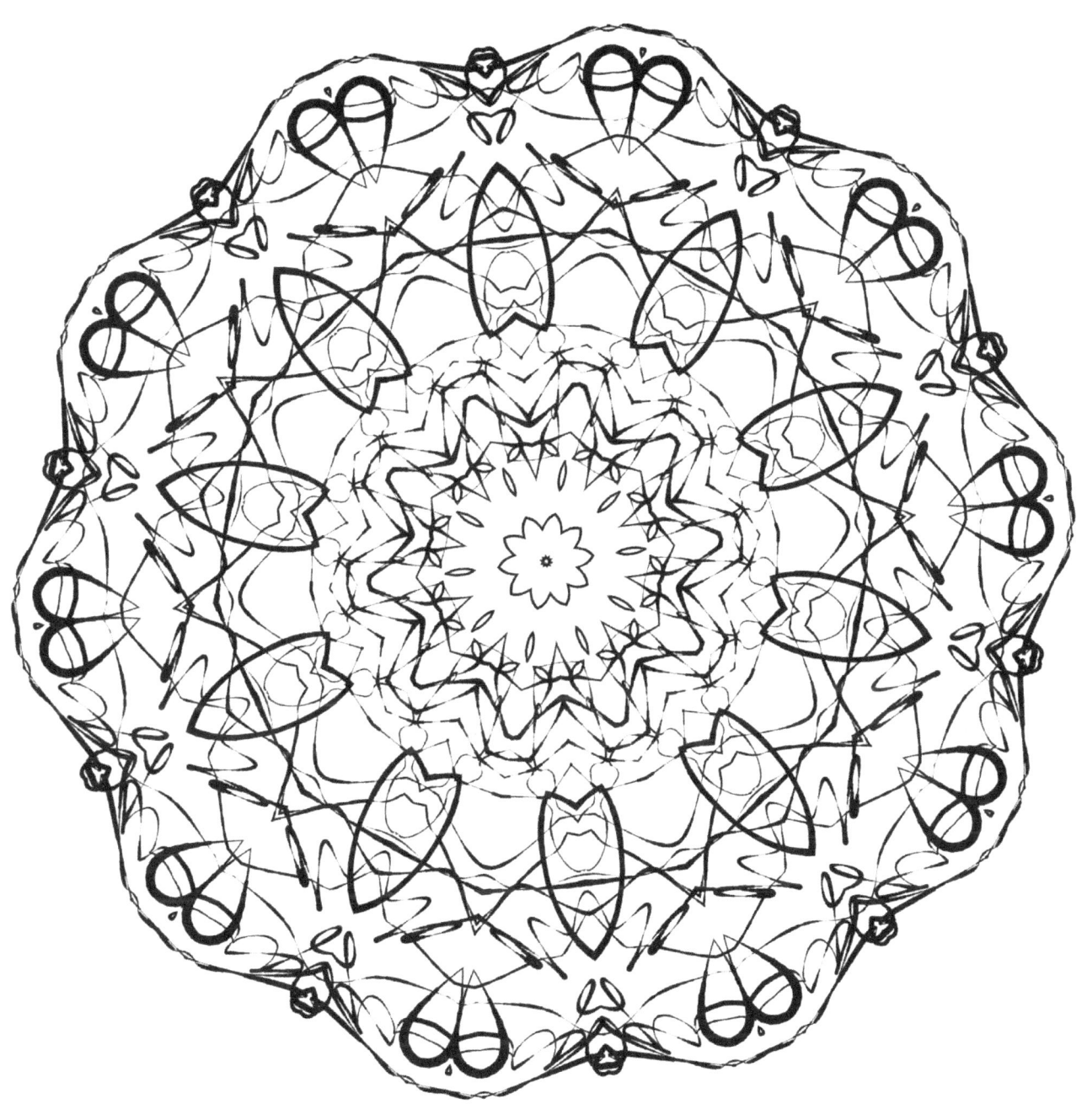

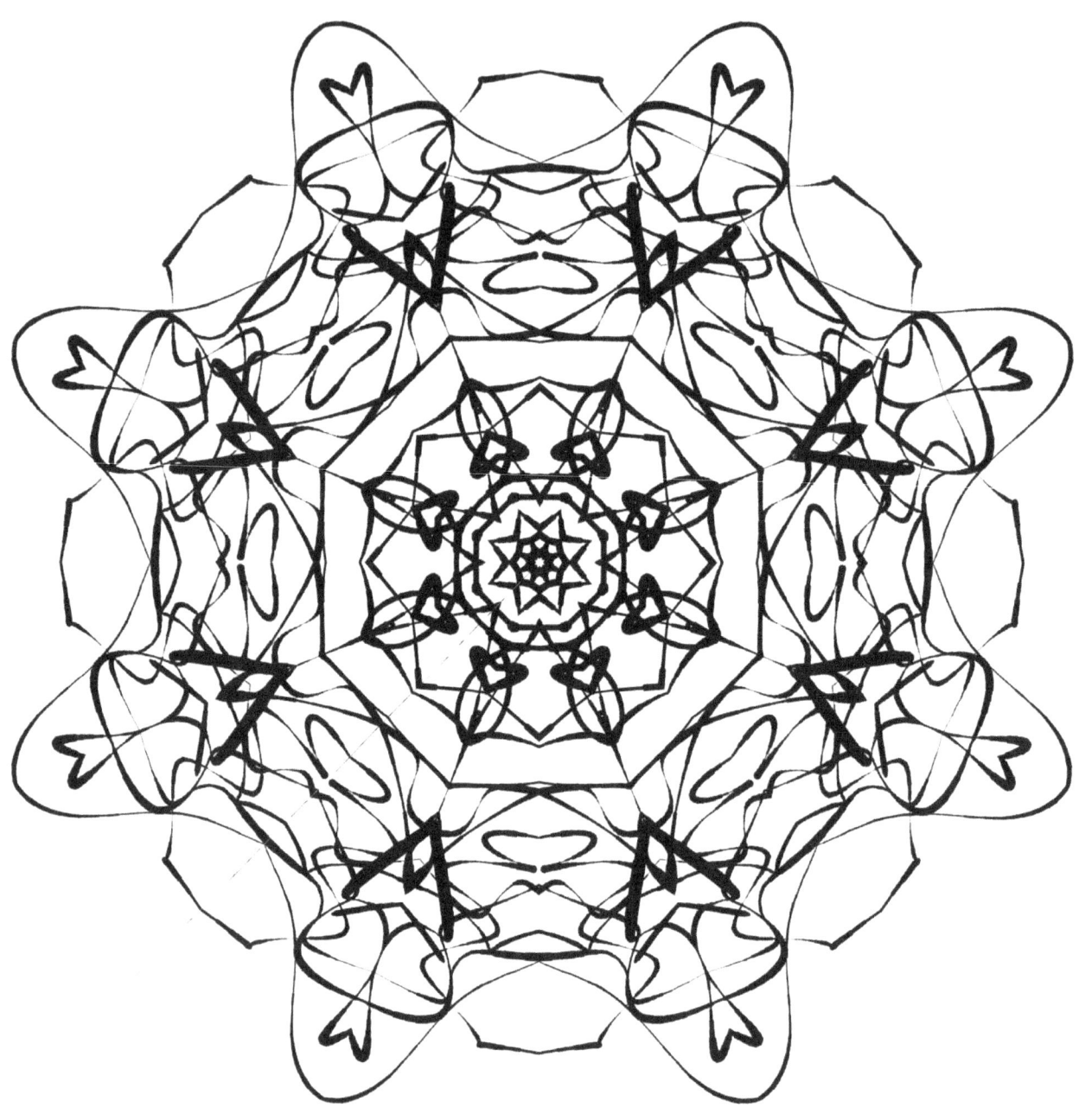

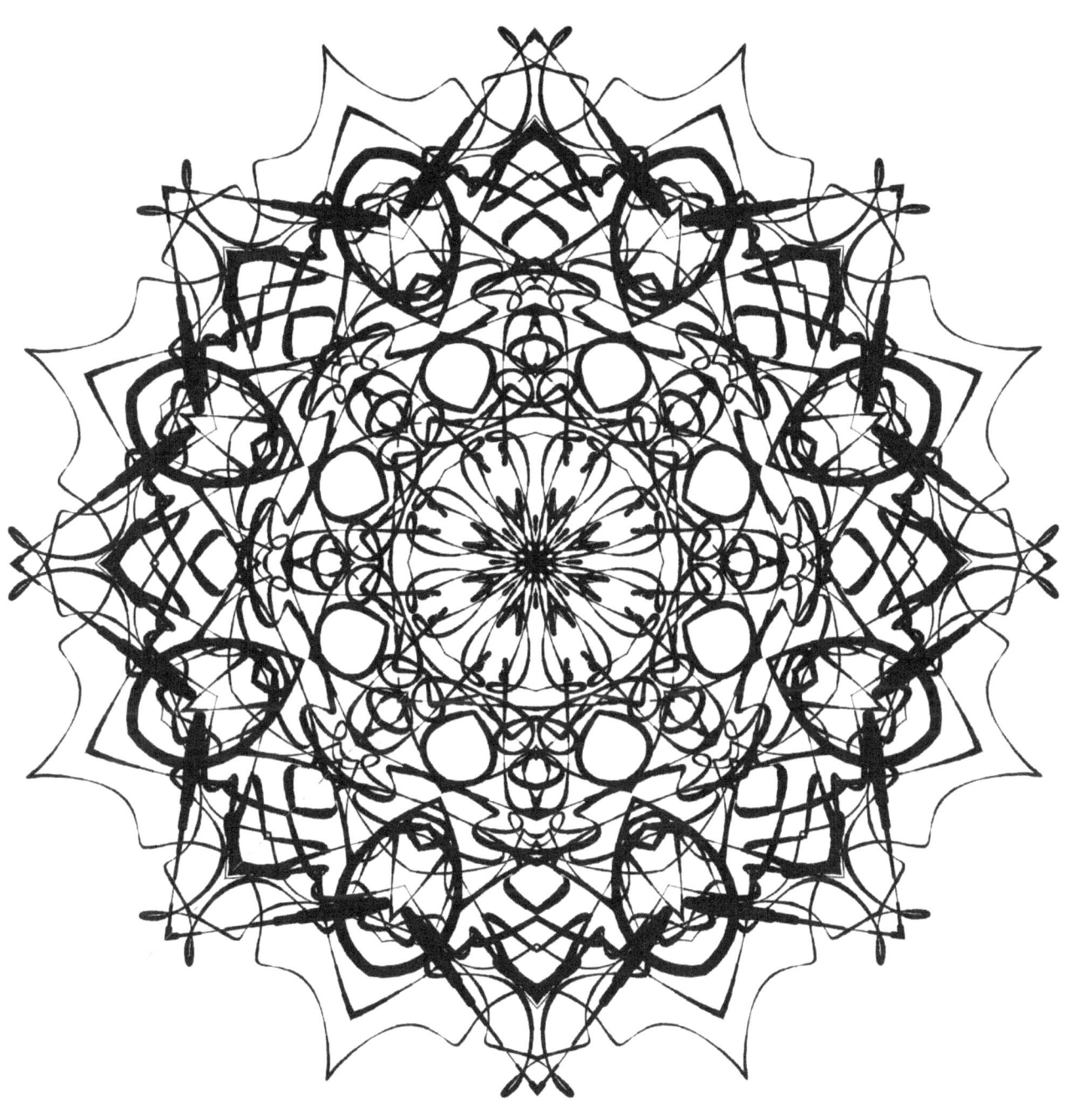

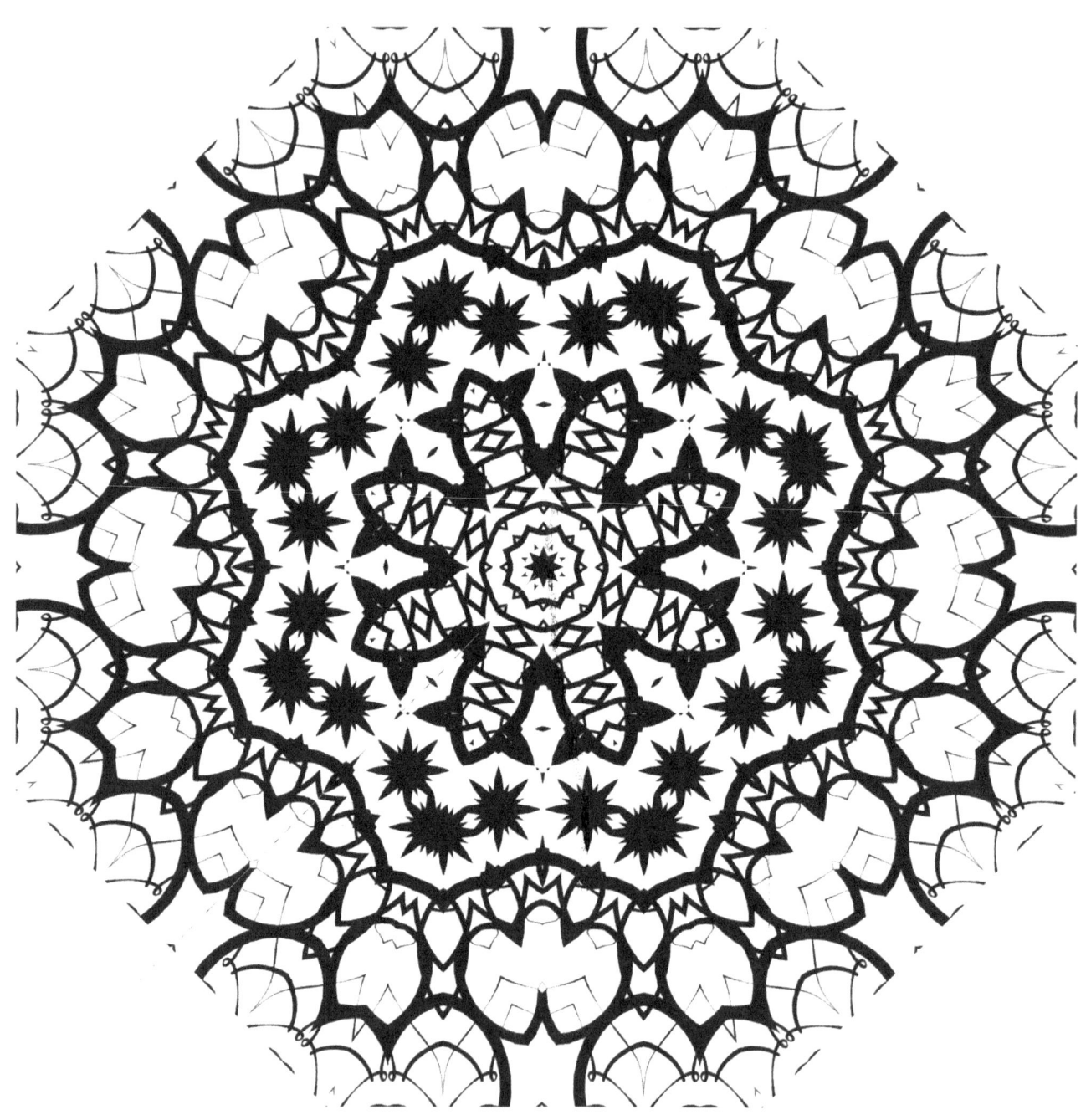